NOTES OF A CONVICT OF 1838

BY

François Xavier Prieur

TRANSLATED BY

GEORGE MACKANESS

ETT IMPRINT
SYDNEY-PARIS LINK

ETT IMPRINT
PO Box R1906

Royal Exchange NSW 1225
Australia

ISBN 978-1-922384-22-6 (paper)
ISBN 978-1-922384-23-3 (ebook)

A Sydney-Paris Link publication,
in memory of Jean-Paul Delamotte

For the details of Francois Prieur's life I desire to thank Dr. Emile Falardeau, of Montreal, Canada, from whose work, *Prieur l'Idéaliste,* by his very kind permission, they were taken.
For assistance in the preparation of this edition of Prieur's *Notes* I am much indebted to Miss L. Leontine Marks, B.A., of Sydney; M. Gaston Derome, Archivist, of Montreal, Canada, and Mrs.M. Edwards, of Croydon, New South Wales, a grand-daughter of Joseph Marceau, one of the "Patriotes". G. MACKANESS.

Design by Hanna Gotlieb
Cover painting: *Battle of Saint-Eustache* by Charles Beauclerk.
Cover design by Tom Thompson.

To M. Gaston Derome
Fervent Chercheur Biographique
Et Généalogique, De Montréal, Canada.

Louis Papineau, the great orator of the "Patriotes."

INTRODUCTION

Two only of the French-Canadian prisoners transported to New South Wales after the rebellion of 1838 left accounts of their experiences during the disturbances, on the voyage out, and in the colony. A translation of one of these, *Journal of a Political Exile in Australia* by Leon Ducharme, Montreal, 1845, is now available The second, entitled *Notes d 'un Condamné Politique de, 1838*, by Francois Xavier Prieur, was first published in the volume entitled *"Les Soirées Canadiennes,"* Receuil de Littérature Nationals, Quatrième Année, issued in Quebec by Brousseau Fréres, in 1864. A new edition, published in Montreal by Cadieux and Derome, appeared in 1884.

FRANCOIS XAVIER PRIEUR

An extract from the Register of Births, Deaths and Marriages of the Parish of St. Joseph, Seigniory of Soulanges, commonly called "Les Cedres," for the year 1814, contains the following particulars concerning the birth of the author of this monograph:-

"On the ninth of the month of May, 1814, by me, Father Soussigné, parish priest of the Parish of Soulanges, was baptised Francois Xavier, born yesterday from the lawful marriage of Antoine Prieur, farmer, of this parish and Archange Véronault, formerly Dennis, his wife."

The godfather was Etienne Marlot, and the godmother Catherine Beauregard, both of whom, apparently, were unable to read or write.

Antoine Prieur is described as a farmer in comfortable circumstances, living in a modest cottage at Soulanges. Both he and his wife, Archange, were devout Roman Catholics with a great love of their native soil. Antoine, on 2nd October, 1809, had married Archange Dennis, formerly Véronneau, or Véronault, the daughter of Pierre and Suzanne Larocque. Antoine was the fourth, Archange the third generation born in Canada.

Less than four years after the birth of Xavier, his parents left Soulanges for the north-eastern forest country of Nouvelle Longueuil, where a new settlement called Saint Polycarpe had been established. The inhabitants of this region made their living chiefly by logging, and transporting to the coast in bark canoes furs collected in the higher regions. Under such conditions the trappers' children learned to swim as soon as they learned to walk, for their favourite amusement was riding the logs being floated down the river towards the St. Laurence. There, on the youthful brain of young Xavier, were engraved the earliest memories of life. He was the pride and joy of his parents. Though fair and blue-eyed as his father, he is said to have been the living image of his mother.

His childhood was passed chiefly in helping his parents, and in the care of his young brothers and sisters, rocking them to sleep with the romantic tales of old France learned from his mother. Like all his companions, he learned to ride the floating logs; sometimes, too, he witnessed accidents, for each year drownings in the river were not uncommon.

On the 15th of July 1827, Xavier was confirmed at Saint Polycarpe by Bishop Lartigue, of Telmesse. He was then thirteen. When the time arrived for him to go to work his health was not robust enough to allow him to brave the perils of a trapper or logger's life. Neither did farming attract him. So, on the advice of the parish priest, his parents found him a position with the principal storekeeper at Soulanges, whose shop was the gathering-place of all the old cronies of the district. From these, with open ears, he learned not only local history, but the more important details of the British conquest of Canada. Thus six years passed, years in which he mastered all the details connected with the buying and selling of the necessities of life.

Small in stature - he measured only five feet four and a half inches - Xavier seemed even younger than his age. In the course of trips with his master he visited the village of Saint Timothée, where, in 1835, he set up his own business, and soon, thanks to hard work, was in control of an important store.

On a matter of business, Prieur chanced to write to Fabres bookshop in Saint Vincent Street, Montreal, where was located the headquarters of an organisation whose aim was the popularisation of a spirit of nationalism amongst the French Canadians. As a result, Prieur there became acquainted with Louis Papineau, the great orator; Duvernay, the popular proprietor of "The Minerva"; La Fontaine; Viger; Rodier; Beaudry; Cartier; Cherrier and other persons not less important politically, with all of whom he became friendly.

When, in 1838, the inevitable crisis occurred, Prieur, by force of circumstances, was sworn in as "Castor" of "L'Association des Chasseurs," founded to drive out of the country the hated English. The narrative of Rapin, one of the leaders, states:

"I replied to those gentlemen who offered me this position of 'Castor' that not having the enthusiasm for this affair that I observed in them, I was, afraid of harming the cause on some particular occasion, through this same lack of enthusiasm, but I told them that I had near me a young and very intelligent storekeeper who, although youthful, would render good service to the cause by his zeal and his activity, meaning F. X. Prieur, who carried on his business about a mile from my home. With common consent M. Prieur was invited, and voluntarily accepted the rank of 'Castor,' [1]

As leader of the rebels for the village of Saint Timothée, Prieur took an active part in all the vicissitudes of the unequal struggle, the full details of which will be found in his own *Notes*, now for the first time printed in English. In his brochure, entitled "Prieur l'Idéalists;" Dr. Emile Falardeau, however, includes the following interesting note:- "Prieur and the other leaders of the rebellion of the Shire of Beauharnais, were sincere and honest in their ideal. They believed that all those who joined them would be in the same category, but they were deceived in their expectation. The leaders were far from suspecting:

"That the noblest of causes have traitors and apostates;

"That, more often than otherwise, crises would serve as pretexts to gratify personal vengeance;

"That people would take advantage of these opportunities to get rid of business rivals more successful than themselves;

"That family interests would place brothers in opposite camps."

"That the Irish element would join the age-old hated enemy; would make common cause with him rather than aid the Canadians in their just claims;

"That these 'gallic vipers' would bite the hands of these kindly disposed people who had sympathised with their wretchedness since their immigration into this country.

"That, through necessity, poor people would become cowardly when tempted by the bait of an unexpected advantage; the offer, for example, of a reward.

"That sentries posted as strategic points, would desert their post without warning their companions of the danger which threatened them;

"That rebels, at the moment of taking aim at the soldiers, would remember the commandment, 'Thou shalt not kill,' and would then fire into the air;

"That traitors would prevent them from carrying out their plans by revealing their activities agreed upon at secret meetings."

The rebellion, from these and other causes, having failed, the patriots of Saint Timothée, like the rest, had to pay the penalty of their actions. Their names were known to the military authorities, who were not in the mood to pardon or forget the offences.

In spite of the fact that Major Denny, the British Commander in that district, promised the rebels immunity if they surrendered, Prieur was suspicious, and on the advice of his friend and confidant, Charles Rapin, decided to attend the meeting that was to be held at the home of Stephen May, the miller. Before doing so, however, he warned his friend that, if treachery were intended, he had decided to seek refuge in the United States.

Word of the meeting having been conveyed to Major Denny, he sent a hundred soldiers, who surrounded the mill and arrested the whole of the "patriots" gathered there. Not one escaped.

After several days' detention, the prisoners were sent, by forced marches, to Montreal, where a hostile crowd greeted them with cries of "Shoot them!" "Hang them!" At "Pied-du-Courant" gaol, Prieur was locked up in the same cell as Charles Hindenlang.

On the 8th January, Prieur and eleven others were informed that their trial would begin three days later. According to Dr. Falardeau, one of the accused, Dr. Perrigo, a foreigner by birth and a veteran of the 1812 rebellion, on entering the court room on the appointed date, gave the Masonic sign of distress which was immediately recognised by the Masons who composed the tribunal. The court was then adjourned, Perrigo being tried separately.

The trial of the other eleven lasted from the 11th to the 21st January, 1839. In the case of Prieur, No.5 on the list, the sentence was death. Though many influential and distinguished citizens pleaded for mercy on behalf of the unfortunate victims, twelve, including De Lorimier, confined in the same cell as Prieur, paid the extreme penalty. Prieur's sentence was commuted to transportation for life to Botany Bay. In his *Notes* Prieur has given a complete account of the sufferings endured by the transportees, both on board the *Buffalo*, and during the years of their residence in New South Wales. Thanks to the activities of the" Association de la Délivrance," a full pardon was eventually granted to all the Patriots of 1838. Of the 58 transported, two, Joseph Dumouchelle and Ignace-Gabriel Chevrefils, died in Sydney; one, Joseph Marceau,[2] married and remained in Australia; 55, including Prieur, ultimately returned to Canada.

A Montreal Newspaper, *Les Mélanges Religieux*, on Tuesday, 15th September, 1846, contained the following paragraphs:-

"ARRIVAL OF A PATRIOT. Mr. F. X. Prieur, whose arrival in London we announced some little time ago, is at last back home in Montreal. He reached here on Tuesday morning by way of Quebec. Mr. Prieur embarked at Sydney on the 22nd last February with a French family who were returning to France, and who paid his passage as far as London, where he disembarked on the 14th June after a voyage of four months and two days. He left London again on the 10th July on the merchantman, *Bilton*, which only arrived at Quebec on Saturday last, after a passage of two months.

"Mr. Prieur left Montreal yesterday morning to visit his family at St. Polycarpe. Before the troubles, Mr. Prieur was a storekeeper at Beauharnais. He is a cultured young man of high intelligence."

On the advice of Mr. Marc-Antoine Primeau, Prieur settled down at Sainte Martine, in the parish of Chateauguay, where, on 17th July, 1849, he married Mrs. Primeau's adopted daughter, Miss Marguerite Aurélie Neveaux, elder daughter of Gédéon Neveaux and of the late Marguerite Roussel.

For several years Prieur continued in business, first at Sainte Martine, and later at Beauharnais, A conservative in politics, he became the intimate friend of the Hon. George Cartier, the Prime Minister, of La Fontaine, and of other important persons belonging to this party. Hearing that Mr. John Glenn, of 200 Saint Paul Street, Montreal, wished to sell his business, Prieur and his good friend Louis Renaud, purchased it, and continued the trade under the title of Renaud and Prieur, importers of crockery and English pottery. In this connection he made several trips to England, where he renewed his acquaintance with Mr. John Roebuck, M.P.[3]

In 1860, recognising Prieur's interest in and devotion to the Conservative party, Cartier appointed him superintendent of the Reformatory at Ile-aux-Noix. When later this institution was transferred to the Saint Vincent de Paul Society it was renamed the Penitentiary. Soon after this, Prieur sold his share in the importing business to Charles Renaud, his partner's son.

About the year 1875, Prieur was appointed Superintendent of all the Canadian prisons. In the course of his duties he travelled through Canada, the United States, and several times crossed the Atlantic to investigate the administration of prison systems.

In 1876 Mrs. Prieur died suddenly while travelling in a train between Ottawa and Montreal. Prieur himself died on 1st January, 1891, aged 76 years and 7 months. Before his death he expressed the wish that two of his companions in exile, Messrs. D. Laberge, then Sheriff of Beauharnais, and F. M. Lepailleur, should be his pall-bearers, a wish that was carried out. He was buried at the cemetery of la Côte des Neiges, Montreal. An account of his funeral will be found in the *Minerva*, of 5th January, 1891.

For ampler accounts of the Rebellion, the reader is referred to the list of references to be found in my Introduction to Ducharme's *Journal*, and to the entries under Ducharme and Prieur in Mr. Justice J. A. Ferguson's *Bibliography of Australia*, Vol. 3, in the press.

1."Castor" is the Canadian huntsman's term for "the beaver".

2. For Marceau's career see note p. 136 following.

3. For John Roebuck's association with the French-Canadian exiles, see Ducharme, *Journal d'un Exilé Politique*," p. 93, and my translation, p. 70.

The Old Man of '37 by Henri Julien, 1880.

Battle of St. Eustache in Lower Canada December 14 1837.
Battle at Montgomery's Tavern, Upper Canada December 7 1837.

FOREWORD

In this volume I make not the slightest claim to the writing of memoirs; still less to a recital of the "troubles" of 1837 and 1838. My title expresses what this book contains; it states that I was convicted, and that I took note of the events in which I played a part, both before and after my exile.

I shall refrain from discussing every reflection, every comment on the revolutionary movements which have characterized the period in question: let me repeat that I do not propose to write history; but that I wish to provide, for those who do, my share of the exact information concerning the things that I have seen with my own eyes, touched with my own hands, and suffered in my own person.

A long time has elapsed since I asked God to pardon me for whatever my personal actions may have contained worthy of censure, for having at that time disobeyed the orders of the church expressed by our early fathers; a long time has also elapsed since I have forgiven all those who have done me wrong. It is, therefore, in a spirit of calm that I write because of the truth that is in me, and I call upon Heaven to stand witness of the purity and good faith of my testimony.

I shall narrate events exactly as they occurred, without the slightest exaggeration, and, especially, without any desire to injure; but with the intention that they may serve as a lesson for those who read them.

These notes begin in the autumn of 1838, the date when I engaged in my first, and, I hope, my last campaign, and end in the autumn of 1846, the date of my return from exile. They have been collected on loose sheets during the course of those long years of misery, during which one thing alone has supported me against the agonies of the heart and the body, against the outbursts of temper; that thing believers will readily recognise, Religion. Thanks, ah, thanks, O God, for having nurtured within the bosom of your Church, one holy and Catholic, and thanks to you, my good old parents, for having inculcated in me its holy tenets.

I have revised these notes, some of which were recorded in the depths of a dungeon, when over me hung the weight of a death sentence; when the dead bodies of some of the companions of my captivity hung suspended from the gibbet ... I have brought a little order into these loose sheets, and since I have little skill in writing, I have communicated them to a friend, who has very kindly undertaken to make in them the correctness in style necessary to make them acceptable to the reader.

I repeat that I speak not merely of what I have known, either directly or indirectly, but from certain knowledge, and I speak of this without rancour, but also without fear; to each one his works for the history and the education of all. Of the causes of the rebellion, of its organisation (if there was any organisation), of the trend of its movements, of the consequences, I shall say nothing. The reader should not be astonished, then, at the purely personal character of the notes taken under the conditions which I have, just stated.

Francois Xavier Prieur

1

Taking the Field

The news, brought during the autumn of 1838, into the parishes of the South-west part of Lower Canada, that an uprising was to take place pretty soon, had created considerable excitement there: help was expected from the United States, and co-operation organized on behalf of Upper-Canada. Each one forgot the disasters of the preceding year in order to dwell only on the possibility of success, and, with it, the cessation of all the distress attributed to political and social causes. I was young and inexperienced, a sincere lover of my homeland; I believed in the existence of all the evils enumerated; in the efficacy of the proposed remedy; I had read something of the heroism of our forefathers; I felt myself of good stock. Enthusiastically I took part in the general training. I joined up with all the faith, all the self-abnegation, all the delight even that one can put into a cause to which one is sincerely devoted.

One thing, however, cast a veil of sadness over my enthusiasm, and that was the opposition of the clergy towards our enterprise. Otherwise I would most probably not be publishing these lines today, for I would in all likelihood be dead, with my weapons in my hand, with many others who thought as I did, though they did not say so.

At this period I was living in the parish of Saint Timothee, where for some little time I had been in business as a merchant. Notified by underground information rather than in any other manner, the friends of the movement, or to employ the word then in common use, which I shall adopt, "the patriots" met from time to time to confer on equipment and other arrangements necessary for an armed rising. Such, at least, was the state of affairs in my own parish, and in those adjacent.

None of us had any exact ideas concerning what was taking place elsewhere, any more than what we had to undertake on our own account; some, impelled by a devotion more generous than enlightened, sustained by those ill-considered connections which come in their train, although one cannot take them much into account, displayed a feverish anxiety, while others, carried away by the example, announced to their assemblies that they would have refused (to take part) had it not been for the fear of being considered bureaucrats. A very small number amongst the French-Canadians dared to condemn the movement straight-out; many, however, refrained from taking part in it, on account of the ban imposed by the clergy, who struggled with admirable courage against the feelings of the time, braving unpopularity both from without and within, subordinating to duty and reason, the sympathies of the heart, the ties of blood, the heartfelt yearnings of love of country and nationality.

The organisation in my parish, in which I had not taken any great part, consisted, quite simply, of the promise of a certain number to muster, under arms, at the call of the leaders, whose names, even then, were widely known. As for our armament, it did not require a long train of vehicles for its transport. Some few hundred cartridges and a small quantity of powder and lead composed our munitions depot. Our artillery park composed only six ironbound, wooden cannon. Our partisan sympathisers were able to collect about a hundred sporting guns; of which the majority dated back to the French period; the others were armed with iron pitchforks in the shape of pikes and scythes transformed into swords.

Thus equipped, minus the cannon which were scarcely adapted to the exigencies of transport, the contingents from the parishes of Sainte Martine, St. Timothée and Beauharnais assembled at the village of Beauharnais on the night of the 3rd or the 4th of November.

At four o'clock in the morning we were assembled there to the number of about 600 men, of whom one half were armed with guns, the other with farming implements converted into instruments of war.

Our campaign was to be launched that very morning by the capture of a steamer (the *Brougham*, I think), which, at this period plied between Lachine and the Cascades. The opinion was expressed that the military authorities would not fail to make use of this boat to transport the troops, and the rumour even spread that this steamer had just been equipped with two guns, supported by a squad of soldiers, so that its use could be assured to the government. It appeared important, therefore, not to postpone until another day the task of making ourselves master of this vessel, and it was resolved to take possession of it that very day, which was that of its journey from Beauharnais down the river to Lachine.

As we were expecting a vigorous resistance, we took greater precautions than would have been necessary in the case of an ordinary trading vessel. Two hours were devoted to making our preparations, and when the steamer appeared, at six o'clock in the morning, this same day, the 4th of November, we had pickets posted in separate parts of the village, about a hundred men in the houses adjoining the wharf, and fifty men, under my command, placed in the shelter of a shed on the wharf itself.

As soon as the boat was tied up to the wharf by its cable, I gave the signal, and rushing forward with all speed, within a minute we were on the deck of the steamer, which, in a very brief time, was invaded by about a hundred and fifty armed patriots.

On board, for soldiers, were only two English officers, charged doubtless, with some mission to which we were not wholly strangers; no resistance was offered to us.

It would be difficult to depict the confusion which took place amongst the passengers, almost all of whom were in bed and asleep when the noise of people's footsteps came and roused them from their slumber. The men, having hastily donned their clothes, asked what was the meaning of all this, and the women, in their night gowns, rushed about imploring pity from all these armed men.

I hastened to get into touch with the captain of the vessel, whom I knew, and to tell him to collect all his people together so as to inform them that no danger was threatening them, neither in respect of their persons nor their property, and to explain to them the cause of this act of violence of which they were accidently the object.

Very soon calm was restored, and when the captain informed me that the passengers had completed their toilet, I went among them to extend to them the hospitality of the patriots' village. Some twenty of the passengers, ladies and gentlemen, including the two officers, were escorted to the house of M. Quintal, the priest, who received them in his kindest manner; the others were lodged at the Hotel Provost, situated near the landing place.

Before the arrival at Beauharnais of the contingents from St. Martine and St. Timothée, the arrest had taken place of the Honourable Mr. Ellice Squire, of Beauharnais, recently arrived from England, and of other persons known to be firm supporters of the government; all had been sent under escort three leagues distant into the parish of Chateauguay.

For myself, I was as concerned as possible about these detentions, but, on the other hand, it must be confessed that they were necessary to the success of the cause that we were defending, and that they constituted, in the circumstances, an essential precautionary measure.

Wishing to render these measures as bearable as possible to the persons concerned, I went to see Mrs. Ellice, who had with her another lady, who, I was told, was her sister, to assure her that her husband and his companions taken prisoners would not be in any danger, and to offer her all the sympathy in our power. These ladies, having expressed the wish to take refuge in the presbytery of Beauharnais, six of the most respectable farmers were appointed to accompany them there, at the same time as we were placing a regular guard at the Manor house, so as to protect the property there from any attack. A messenger was allotted to Mrs. Ellice, so that she could communicate with her husband, and every day our prisoners exchanged news with the ladies of their families left behind at Beauharnais ; in a word, everything possible was done which could prove to the families the respect and sympathy of which they were the object.

This is the place for me to pay to my fellow-countrymen this tribute: that from the midst of this mob suddenly in arms, entirely lacking in organization and recognised authority, no disorder emanated ; no one dishonoured the cause that we regarded as great and just.

Posts were set up in various places, to prevent a surprise attack from without, and to protect the families and property of persons of British origin, known at Tories or Bureaucrats, and held prisoners at Chateauguay, or in the Hotel Provost. That having been done, we kept on waiting for the orders that we expected continually to receive from the Provisional Government, which we had been informed, was being set up on the frontiers.

Round about two o'clock on the same day, a messenger brought us an order, written, he told us, in the hand of Dr. Robert Nelson, and sent by Drs. Nelson and Cote, instructing us to hold ourselves in readiness to march within two hours of reception of the notice, towards a point which would shortly be indicated to us.

The remainder of this first day of campaigning and the succeeding night passed as quietly as possible.

Round about ten o'clock on the morning of the 5th, a messenger from Chateauguay brought us the news that the leaders of this parish, including Messrs Cardinal and Duquette, had just been arrested. These arrests had been made by natives of Sault Saint Louis, commanded by Mr. George de Lorimier. By one of those coincidences so frequent during revolutions, we had in our midst at this moment in Beauharnais the unfortunate Chevalier de Lorimier, later condemned to death and executed, a member of the same family which had just displayed so strong a proof of its zeal for the opposite cause.

These arrests had created alarm in the minds of a good number of respectable old families, who, having probably never had any great confidence in the organization of the Insurrection, seeing themselves commanded for the most part by young and inexperienced men, foresaw immediate fatal consequences from a movement thus concerted and carried out. A deputation from among them came and addressed themselves to the unfortunate Chevalier de Lorimier and to myself with the proposal that we should seek out the Honourable Mr. Ellice so as to make him a protector on behalf of the Government and voluntarily lay down our arms ill his presence.

To these fine fellows I replied that no one was compelled to act with us, that the liberation of Mr. Ellice would not have the effect that they anticipated, and that, as far as I, myself, was concerned, I could not assume any responsibility for such an act, without knowing what result it might have on the fate of those who were relying upon our co-operation, and to whom this co-operation was promised.

Up to this time, Mr. de Lorimier had not taken any active part in the movement, at least, as far as I was personally aware. When my reply was conveyed to the person whom I have just mentioned, the action that they were purposing was abandoned, and each one from that time on, accepted in a spirit of resignation the consequences of whatever situation might eventuate.

During the night of the 5th-6th, it was reported that the troopers of the Sault Saint Louis were advancing against the village of Beauharnais. It was about two o'clock in the morning, the night being extremely dark. The call to arms was immediately made, and as soon as we were assembled, which was within a moment or two, we set out to meet the enemy. But it was a false alarm, and after a difficult and tiring march, we returned to our quarters.

During our sojourn in the village, the women and children belonging to the farmers of the parish brought us provisions which we prepared as best we could, and we lodged by squads in the various houses and buildings of the village.

On the 6th I received an invitation to dine on board the steamer; this came from the captain, Mr. Wipple, then a prisoner on parole with his crew. I accepted the invitation, and this was the first peaceful and comfortable meal that I had had for several days. The whole day of the 6th was one of anxiety. We received no news from any locality except from Chateauguay, where our friends were losing heart through having lost their leaders, and from lack of knowledge of what was happening elsewhere.

On the 7th, round about two o'clock in the afternoon, there arrived a messenger from the camp of the Patriots, called Baker's, from the name of the spot occupied by this camp on the banks of the River Chateauguay, three leagues distant from Beauharnais. Baker's Camp comprised about three hundred men and the messenger came to ask for help, informing us that a party of eight hundred men, made up of regular troops and volunteers, under the command of Major Campbell,[1] was marching upon them.

Straightaway, and in succession, we reviewed our troops, and taking with us two hundred men, the Chevalier de Lorimier and I set out to march with all speed towards Baker's Camp. The remainder of our troops then assembled at Beauharnais, in accordance with the arrangements made, was to remain there under the command of Messrs. Wattier and Roy until the arrival of fresh orders.

We reached Baker's Camp about six o'clock in the evening, as the result, so one might describe it, of a forced march carried out by all our men with as much cheerfulness as strength and courage. We found our friends standing on guard, protected against any surprise by pickets and sentinels thrown out in every direction. Thus passed the night of the 7th to 8th.

On the 8th, towards nine o'clock In the morning, some of the sentries, at the changing of the guard, came and informed us that the troops were advancing and soon we could distinguish them, without ourselves being seen, at about a quarter of a league distant where they had halted.

Apparently these troops were very tired, for they did not stir during the whole of this Clay, not even to make any reconnaisances in our direction. The whole of this day and the night of the 8th to the 9th passed watching the enemy and in disposing our troops for the now imminent battle between ourselves-strangers to the art of war, and very ill-equipped with arms and a troop superior in numbers, well disciplined and armed to the teeth.

As our commander (in chief) we had elected Dr. Perrigo, a veteran of the Militia of 1812, who was to find us, in respect of discipline and equipment, very different from what our fathers were, those powerful, trained regular militiamen, who, just a quarter of a century previously, had won that famous victory, so well known, on the banks of this same River Chateauguay.

At this moment we were about to march against that same flag that our fathers defended at that time. However, we, too, were about to fight for our native land and all the memories of the glorious past, and all the struggles of our small body of people seemed bound in this moment of apparent weakness and of discouraging circumstances, to take for us the place of arms and a flag.

The Insurgents, at Beaunharnais, Lower Canada 1838 by Katherine Jane Ellice.

2

During and After the Fight

On the 9th November, about nine o'clock in the morning, some men on picket duty came and warned us that the enemy was advancing. Shouts of joy within our ranks welcomed this news, and the order was immediately given for us to draw up in battle array to await the coming of the enemy. Our Commander, Dr. Perrigo, after having given his orders, went away to make sure that nothing was threatening us in the rear, and to see that everything was set in order in the camp; he had not yet returned when we saw the enemy debouching along the main road. Such was the enthusiasm of our men and so great their desire to come to close quarters that, without waiting for their commander, they asked Mr. Nevue, one of our officers, to place himself at our head and to take command, which he, as impatient as the others, did, crying out, in his thunderous tones, and from the top of his tall stature: "Forward!"

To this shout our five hundred voices replied with an "hurrah"; then at once we made a rush across the fields in the direction of the troops, calling out: "Victory!"

We rushed upon the enemy, enfilading him and discharged a round which could not have had any great effect being fired from too great a distance; but of which the noise added to the yells that our companies uttered, as soon as they appeared, and of whose numbers the enemy was wholly unaware, and that undoubtedly they exaggerated, had the effect of creating a certain amount of panic and of which we took advantage to reload our weapons without relaxing our cries and scarcely retarding our course. A general but ill-directed volley by the troopers caused a shower of bullets to whistle above our heads, of which not a single one struck us. No more than did any of the succeeding volleys. During this time we continued to advance, across ploughed fields, ditches and fenced paddocks, firing at will, but with a certain amount of effect, as we discovered a little later.

Finally we were about to come to close quarters with the enemy, when a last volley, accompanied by redoubled shouts, succeeded in demoralizing them, and we saw them take to flight, carrying off two dead and several wounded, according to what we ourselves noticed and the information which we received later from the folk in the vicinity. Our forces were already along the road in pursuit, when Dr. Perrigo, who had rejoined us at the sound of the first volley, advanced to the front rank and gave the order to stop.

There is no doubt that our commander feared, and rightly, an offensive reprisal by soldiers armed with bayonets against our men who were without them; probably, too, he could not fathom the precipitate retreat of the troopers otherwise than by supposing that in this movement there was a ruse contrived to lead us to a hand-to-hand conflict, carried out with totally unequal weapons. Whatever may have been the opinions of our leader, and the cause of the enemy's retreat, it was only with great regret that we obeyed our commander's order, and several of us, including the Chevalier de Lorimier, immediately addressed to him some pointed reproofs.

The enemy, who numbered some hundreds of men, but not eight hundred as we had been told, watched by certain men charged with this task, was now well in retreat. We returned, therefore, to our residential quarters at the camp, of which the sleeping places were the houses and barns of Messrs. Baker, Valeé and other farmers settled at the fork of the four roads.

This particular day was a cold one, with a little snow. The dreariness of the atmosphere harmonized with our dissatisfaction at not having derived any profit from a victory, gained without any sacrifice on our part, and which would have been able, in our opinion, to provide us with arms and munitions in abundance.

Just as evening approached, a messenger came and brought us the unpleasant news of the defeat of our friends from Lacolle and the Côtes; he added that many had been taken prisoner, and that the news everywhere was bad.

It was evident that our position was becoming untenable, and that to remain longer assembled in this place meant merely to attract disaster to the spot, without any possible good result for the cause that we were defending. The whole of the night from the 9th to the 10th was spent in discussion; we agreed then that the day following the victory might be a very unhappy one for us.

It was agreed that those who were not deeply involved should return quietly to their homes; that the others, under the orders of the Chevalier de Lorimier should make for the frontier, almost fifteen leagues distant, whilst I should return, with my company, to Beauharnais, to confer there with our friends who had remained in that village.

I arrived at Beauharnais between 10 and 11 o'clock in the morning. There I found two hundred and forty men all under arms; the rest of them, after a week's absence - a fairly long period for a Canadian farmer - had gone home to visit their families. Discouragement could be read on every face. It caused us to consider deeply, when dwelling on the total absence of organization and of ways and means, on the certain and useless dangers into which so many families were running, and on the thought that, probably at this very moment, we were the only ones under arms. In spite of everything, as we had not received any orders to put an end to all attempt at resistance, we resolved to hold out as long as possible.

At three o'clock in the afternoon, a messenger came to inform us that an army corps of men, estimated to number 1200, composed of regulars and volunteers from Glengarry, and reported to be dragging with them six pieces of artillery had crossed the stream at the foot of Lake St. Francis and was marching upon Beauharnais. When this news was received we began hastily to make our arrangements for marching to meet the forces without even considering at the moment, the madness I must confess, of such an idea. I ordered a certain number of men to guard the village and our prisoners, and we set out at once to march towards St. Timothée (my own parish), through which the troopers were coming, dragging with us four wooden cannon, mounted on improvised gun carriages.

I had sent ahead, post haste, a party of men charged with the duty of watching the movements of the enemy, and of destroying a bridge situated on a deep gully which cuts across the road between the parishes of St.

Timothée and Beauharnais. We met this party three quarters of a league from the village of Beauharnais; it reported to us that the troopers were in action on the bridge from the time of its arrival at this spot, and that consequently little time would elapse before they would appear before us, for at that moment we were only a half hour's march from this bridge.

At the place where we then were, the road skirts the St. Laurence River, and on the other side, happens to run along the side of a strong stone wall; the road, confined thus between the river and the wall, described a semi-circle: we resolved to await the enemy near this wall, from behind the shelter of which we could open upon its serried ranks a raking fire, at the moment when the column began to describe the semi-circle formed by the road which they must follow.

The weather was cold; night was already beginning to fall.

There we were on our knees on the frozen soil, guns on hips, telling our beads, after having repeated the litanies together. Already could be heard the noise of the heavy vehicles and of the cavalry which were advancing slowly and heavily upon the hard road, when Captain Roy came to me, and, addressing himself to us all, told us it was madness to wish to make any sort of attempt with this handful of ill-armed men, that to begin an impossible resistance was merely to spill blood uselessly, and to bring down on our parishes the vengeance of a powerful and implacable enemy; he proposed that we should abandon all idea of attacking the troops.

I could not refuse to admit the justice of his argument, and he gave the order to disarm. Each one then reconciling himself to the inevitable, made his way across the fields to his own residence.

Having withdrawn, with a certain number of men, some acres away from there, I could catch a glimpse of the troopers filing off into the dark-ness of the oncoming night. The noise of their passage was not yet lost in the distance, so that the blackness, now complete, permitted us to see, in the direction of St. Timothée, the glow of the fires that the troops had lit on their journey.

The reader must conjure up, for I am not capable of expressing it, what was then passing in my mind. For some time, I remained plunged deep in thought, in which grief and anger, forgiveness and vengeance, regret and desire overwhelmed my heart and my senses.

At last, religious feelings prevailing, I resigned myself to the inevitable, and my comrades and I began to ask ourselves, "What are we going to do?" I was more deeply involved than any of them, but I had no family. I proposed crossing over into the United States. All the others replied that they must watch over their families while at the same time they advised me to set out for a foreign land. We shook hands with aching hearts, and full of apprehension, each one for the others, and each one for himself, we scattered so that we should run into less danger, and also because we had to follow different routes.

Here ends my career as a soldier, and as company commander, and begins that of fugitive, of accused committed for trial, of prisoner condemned to death, and of exile amongst convicts.

I do not know whether the reader will be much interested in the history of eight years of misery and suffering of every kind; though, for myself personally it is not without some extreme pleasure that I live them all over again in my memory ... My motives were pure, and without regrets; I have been neither cowardly nor cruel; I have in no way acted dishonestly; I have suffered patiently, and if I sometimes feel indignation, I can with perfect confidence do myself the justice to say I cherish no feelings of hate.

In expiation of my sins I offer to God the misfortunes that I have suffered; to my beloved country I offer them as proof of the love that I have always held for it, and that I still hold. The preceding pages will make other people and particularly young folk, see the danger of being carried away by the enthusiasm of a patriotism which, to the people in control, during a more advanced age, does not imply such a whole-hearted feeling of responsibility as that which weighs upon those who support popular insurrections.

3

Outlaw and Fugitive

Since I had to pass through the parish of St. Timothée in order to make my way into the United States, I decided to pay a brief visit to my own home.

It was very close to eleven o'clock in the evening when I found myself facing the still smoking ruins of my new home, totally destroyed, and that after having met on my way other ruins caused by soldiers who had set fire to several occupied houses and barns stocked with grain. No one was to be met with on the road; the unlighted houses seemed anxious to hide the fears of the women, the children and the accused whom they harboured. I did not dare to approach and knock at the door of any of them for fear of adding to their terrors, of compromising the others, and of exposing myself to the danger of being taken by surprise.

I continued then, alone and sad at heart, in the middle of the night, to walk along the hard road of exile.

Less than half a league from the ruins of my home was situated the house of one of my intimate friends, engaged, like myself, in the revolutionary movement. I went in ... the family was in tears; its head had been taken prisoner by the volunteers that very afternoon and led away to Beauharnais with the troopers who some few hours previously were about to attack us.

"Oh, good heavens! It's you," exclaimed the poor wife of my friend, as soon as she saw me. "Escape, Escape! They are looking for you, and they say they intend to hang you if they catch you ... and my poor husband," she added, bursting into tears.

I felt myself more overcome in the presence of these tears than I had been before the ruins of my house and at my future prospects, and I felt colder, near the fire of this home than in the frosty night along the road.

I did not wish to expose any longer than was necessary, this family to the terrors and dangers arising from my presence in their midst; so I hastened to ask for something to eat so that I could depart immediately; I had eaten nothing since the morning. I ate with very little relish and drank a bowl of milk which did me good; then I took leave of my hosts, as though I should never see them again.

The emotions of these scenes, on top of a six leagues march, and added to the fatigue undergone during the preceding week, during which period I had not once had my clothes off to go to sleep, had at the moment when I saw myself alone again upon the high road amidst the darkness of the night, such an effect on me that I felt myself totally incapable of continuing my journey. I fell to the ground through exhaustion, and I felt my head going round as in a whirl.

I made my way towards a barn, and making use of a ladder that I threw back into its place after I had climbed up, I reached the hayloft, where, hollowing myself out a bed in the hay, I settled down as best I could, and immediately fell into a heavy sleep.

When I awoke, the sun was just rising, but I had not the faintest idea of how long I had been asleep. It was only with difficulty that I was able to account for my position, and I was so numb that I could scarcely move. It took me at least half an hour before I could move my limbs and collect my thoughts. Then, having no other means of getting down, I jumped from a height of about twelve feet on to the frozen earthen floor. I picked myself up, all bruised, and with much difficulty again began my march, directing my steps towards a little wood, which separated the lands of the second concession from those of the river concession.

I passed through this little wood and the clearings of the second concession, so as to reach a forest several leagues distant, in the direction of the frontier. All day long I walked through this forest, sometimes crossing pools of water where the ice broke under my feet, having no compass, and knowing nothing of woodcraft; in the evening I stopped at a sugar hut, where I passed the night, at one time lying on some fir branches that I had gathered, at another walking round the hut to keep myself warm. I did not wish to go to sleep for fear I might not be able to get up again.

At daybreak I resumed my march, and having walked all day, I found myself again at a place through which I had passed the previous evening. Bruised, soaked through, worn out through fatigue and hunger, broken-spirited, I threw myself down at the foot of a tree, there to await death. Commending my soul to my Creator, I pulled out of my jacket pocket a little prayer-book, which had not left me since first I took the field, and began to read, as a preparation for my great journey into Eternity.

I had scarcely began my prayers than I heard in the distance the sound of a woodman's axe: I directed my steps towards the locality from which the noise was coming, and very soon arrived there, without being seen, quite close to a sturdy settler who had recently come into the parish, whose name I did not know, but who knew me: he dropped his axe in surprise when he saw me.

"It is you, Mr. Prieur?" he exclaimed.

I related to him my adventures in the wood, and asked him what was the day of the week. He informed me that it was Tuesday, the 13th November. It was not until then that I realized that I had slept more than thirty hours amongst the hay; that is to say from about midnight on the Saturday until sunrise on Monday morning.

The poor but honest settler told me that a Mr. Brown, a magistrate, was having a search made for me, and that all those who gave me shelter were threatened with imprisonment and the destruction of their property by fire.

The house, or rather, the hut of the settler, for he was then only beginning to establish his home, was somewhat less than a league from the spot where we were; as I did not wish to subject him to any risk, he being the father of a young family, dependent exclusively upon his work for their maintenance, I asked him to be so very kind as to go and find me something to eat; I had eaten nothing for almost three days. He went away and returned within a couple of hours with some barley, a bottle of milk, coffee and some bread.

Becoming aware then of how exhausted I was, and noticing the state of my clothes, and especially of my footwear, this worthy man insisted that I should follow him to his hut to dry my clothes, to warm myself and to have a sleep. "I shall stand guard around my house," he said, "and I promise you that no one will approach without your being warned in time."

I accepted the invitation of my excellent compatriot. After having taken off all my outer garments and my boots and stockings, of which the worthy wife of this worthy man immediately took the greatest care, I threw myself down on a buffalo skin coat beside a very warm stove and went to sleep.

I had made my host promise to wake me at the expiration of three hours; this he did. During those three hours, he had kept, round his dwelling, the most faithful guard that has ever been kept over the life of one of his fellow human beings ....Splendid friend, may God bless him, him and his family, and may his noble action be added in the memory of the Canadians to all those which have brought honour to our race. I was in such a state of confusion at the time that I did not think of asking my host for his name; it has been impossible to discover it since.

I dressed myself and had something to eat, although I was not noticeably hungry (I had a slight touch of fever) ; then my generous host set me on a footpath which led towards St. Timothée, accompanying me on the way for some time.

I made my way back towards St. Timothee because I realized the impossibility of my reaching the frontier by going through the forest. My next plan was to try to link up with someone as interested as myself in escaping towards the United States by going up Lake Saint Francis in order to take the road of exile by water.

I reached the edge of the wood on the morning of the 14th November. Not wishing to approach houses in daylight, I had to wait the whole day long on the outskirts of the wood, with ice cold rain falling, for the return of night. I resumed my journey about nine o'clock in the evening, and a little later, knocked at the dwelling of a farmer whom I knew. The owner came to the door and asked me my name, which I refused to give him; the door opened to receive me.

On learning who I was, my host's wife allowed an involuntary exclamation of fear to escape her: "My God! What's going to become of us!" I was an object of terror even amongst my own people. The gallant farmer immediately replied, "Whatever happens will please God; but we certainly shall not allow him to die for lack of help." His wife then began to prepare me a meal.

After I had eaten I was offered a bed. "But," I said to my generous compatriots, "my presence compromises you, and I would not, for anything in the world be the cause of any harm falling on you."

"We intend to keep watch," replied Mr. Hurtubise (that is the name of my host), "so that nothing unpleasant may happen either to you or to us,"

That night I slept in a good bed, prepared with the care which all our good Canadian housewives give to their works, and at three o'clock in the morning, I again set off, with the intention of reaching the neighbourhood of the river. I took refuge in the hay loft of a barn, where I remained hidden for nearly two days, without daring to allow anyone to suspect my presence. On the second day, ravenous with hunger, I made myself known to a man of my acquaintance, a servant in the employ of the owner of the barn in which I had sought refuge.

To this man I appeared as a ghost coming from another world; he stood stock still for some moments without the power to utter a word. Then, having regained his composure. "Why, it's you!" he said "They are looking for you everywhere. All your property has been burnt, and Mr. Brown has put a price on your head."

I impressed the necessity for silence on my interlocuter, begging him to inform his master, but no one other than his master, that I was on his property, and to bring me something to eat. The good fellow returned very quickly and told me that his master was not at home, and brought, too, an ample supply of bread and milk.

The following morning, the landowner came to me, gave me some information, and told me that my presence there constituted a grave danger both for himself and his family. I begged him to allow me to occupy his barn, until I could see three friends, whose names I gave to him, at the same time praying him to be so good as to warn them, and to arrange a rendezvous for us at an isolated spot, but one not too far from where I was.

At sunset the landowner returned and announced that the persons whom I wished to see would be found at a place that he mentioned, round about nine o'clock in the evening. In fact I met my three friends at the time and place indicated.

They declared to me that my scheme was impracticable; that there was no means of ascending the stream at this time of the year; that the river and the lake were in places covered with ice-floes; but one of them, Mr. Héneault, a young man like myself, who lived with his worthy mother, offered me the hospitality of his house, so that there I might be able to regain my health and strength already much impaired, and await there a favourable opportunity of crossing the river to the northern shore where I could be safer.

I have never ceased to remember with gratitude the kindness that I owe to this good friend, and I hope that he will accept the renewed expression of it which I tender to him here. In the home of Mr. Héneault I received the welcome of a brother, and from his noble mother a reception such as my own mother would have given me had I been under the paternal roof. (My good parents were residing then, as they still do, at Saint Polycarpe.) It was on the 18th of November, about midnight, that I crossed the threshold of this hospitable dwelling.

Hitherto, I have only had an opportunity to pay tribute to the generosity, the devotion, the benevolence and the hospitality showered upon me by various families during these terrible days; all those that I have so far mentioned, their wives and their children have kept my secret which not one of them has betrayed or even allowed to leak out. Now, however, I shall have the unhappy task of setting forth the other side of these noble actions. The most holy causes have their apostates and their traitors, the most chivalrous nations have their renegades ... we have had ours.

Some individuals, whom I will not mention by name, because, in the first place, I have forgotten them, and next, because I do not wish to blacken further with infamy the name that their children bear, children I hope who will be better than they. Certain individuals, formerly my comrades in arms, had got into touch with Major Denny, of the regular army, who commanded a detachment stationed in the vicinity; they had revealed certain information and had obtained from the latter, so it appears, the promise of an immediate pardon if they succeeded in discovering my hiding place.

These wretches, having chosen me as their victim, had laid to my account almost the whole responsibility for the movement, in order to give greater value to their act, and thereby to assure to themselves a much greater guarantee that they should secure their own pardon. The traitors had no difficulty in discovering my retreat, seeing that no one was challenged; so, on the 20th of November, in the morning, my generous hosts and I saw the house invested by soldiers into whose hands I delivered myself without delay so that I might riot any longer or in any greater degree compromise my friend and his aged mother.

Sir John Colborne, Commander in Chief of all British troops in North America and Administrator of Lower Canada..

4

A Prisoner

I was taken before Major Denny, who, on learning my age, saw at once that my person had not all the importance that had been given to it by those who had just been trafficking in my blood; in addition, because he suspected some deception on their part, or perhaps, wishing to save face, he had the wretched informers arrested.

The flour mill at Beauharnais had been converted into a temporary gaol, and there I was taken. In this place we found collected some forty accused, among whom were the aforesaid traitors, whose infamous behaviour no one then suspected. The prisoners occupied the second floor of the mill, which entirely lacked heating, in spite of the very severe cold of the latter part of November; they were placed on a diet of dry bread and water.

I had not been more than a few minutes in the midst of my fellow-prisoners than I was taken into custody again and led into another part of the mill, the miller's own quarters, which place, I was then told, was intended for my temporary prison. I did not know to what I could attribute this special treatment, which in the circumstances, was a very great favour. But the miller told me a little later that I owed this favour to the intercession of certain influential people of the village who wished to recognize the kindness I had shown them previously when Beauharnais was in the power of the patriots. I begged the miller to be so good as to thank sincerely for me these worthy people. During this transitory incarceration, I received visits and messages of consolation from several of our former prisoners, and I take the opportunity here of thanking them, amongst whom was Mrs. Wilson, whose good offices I shall never forget.

On the fourth day after my arrest, in the morning, I was taken again up to the second floor, where I again found my former companions, but a greater number of them; for every day fresh arrests were being made. We were still without a fire, but the ration of food was changed: we were given a little meat and the Canadian families in the village were permitted to supply us with provisions.

Father Quintal, the parish priest of Beauharnais, paid us a visit, and saw that we were supplied with some comforts. It was also through his kindly intervention that a few days later we were able to secure a stove. It was just in time, for we were suffering horribly from the cold.

May I be permitted here to introduce a thought which does my heart good, me, a child of the Catholic Church, a thought concerning the part taken by the priest. At the beginning of that terrible month of November, 1838, the village of Beauharnais was in the power of the rebels, the friends of the Government were prisoners and in fear of their lives; the priest, who was there, protected them, and for them the greatest favour, although they were Protestants, was to be permitted to take shelter beneath the roof of the presbytery . . . . At the end of this same month of November, the same village is in the power of the English troops, and the patriots, in their turn, are prisoners; it is still the same priest who protects these other prisoners, and ameliorates the hardships of their harsh captivity.

The arrests continued; then one day we were informed that, as the Montreal gaol was overflowing with accused persons, our trial was to take place at Beauharnais, were preparations were being made to erect the scaffold destined for the execution of those most guilty.

The same magistrate of whom I have already spoken, had, I do not know by what authority, ordered all the Canadians to come forward and to surrender all the arms that they had in their possession; a certain number obeyed this order, and the arms were immediately smashed under the eyes of those who gave them up. This man was particularly relentless in his treatment of the family of a resident of the village of Beauharnais, Mr. Provost. Not content with having brought about the arrest of the head of this family, whose possessions had been destroyed by fire, he also continued to persecute his poor wife, who, burdened with three children, was compelled to wander from house to house, seeking a refuge, from which her tormentor very soon hunted her away. It was a colonel of the regular army, Colonel Gray, who put an end to this vengeful savagery, by assigning a dwelling to this unfortunate family. May honour be accorded to this worthy soldier.

On the 1st of December, after we had been made to undergo an interrogation, we were chained together, two by two, to the number of fifty-two, almost all fathers of families, and we set out for Montreal under an escort. It was snowing a little and was very cold. In the afternoon we were transported in boats from the village of Sault Saint Louis to La Chine, where we arrived round about five o'clock in the evening. We were lodged in a shed, without a fire, there to spend the night.

On our arrival at La Chine, we had a visit from certain people who informed us that Cardinal Duquette and several others were at that very moment undergoing their trial, and that they were to be put to death at once: Some of the volunteers also threatened us with a similar fate.

During the evening, Mrs. Papin, of La Chine, accompanied by her daughters, came and brought with them some food prepared by their own charitable hands, and gave us many kind words of sympathy and consolation for which God will reward them at the day of recompense for their good deeds.

On the following morning we set out on our journey for Montreal, escorted by some soldiers from a Scottish regiment, whose musicians annoyed us during almost the whole of the journey with the noise of their bagpipes.

On our entry into the suburb of Recollets, this music gave place to a stream of insults, curses and threats, organised by a hostile mob whose cries of "Shoot them! Hang them !" accompanied us as far as La Pointe-à-Callieres, where we were quartered in a shed erected within the prison, where already a large number of prisoners were crowded together. The windows had been boarded up, latrines erected without connexion to the sewer, and stoves installed for cooking food … It is easy to imagine what sort of air we had to breathe in this wretched hole.

On the third day of our detention in this place, Mr. Saint-Ours, then Sheriff of Montreal, paid us a visit, and, seeing the deplorable condition in which we were, took upon himself the responsibility of removing from the windows the barricades which prevented the passage both of air and of light; in this way we procured a little of both those elements so essential for existence.

Several of us lived for five weeks in this dreadful prison. I must here place on record the. humanitarian services rendered by one of the prison warders named Devillerais, who, during the little free time allowed him by his laborious duties, was kind enough to go out and buy for us food for which, owing to the poverty of the regulation daily allowance, we stood greatly in need.

On the 8th December, we got word of the condemnation to death of some of our friends whose names were, Joseph Narcisse Cardinal, Solicitor; Joseph Duquette, Law Student; Francois Maurice Lepailleur, Sherriff's Officer; Jean Louis Thibert, Jean Marie Thibert, Joseph Lécuyer, farmer; Leandre Ducharme, commercial traveller; Joseph Guimond, Louis Guerin and Antoine Côte, farmers. The argument at the trial of these patriots had continued from the 28th of November. These ten days had seemed over long drawn out according to certain English newspapers: it will be recalled that some of these wrote that it was not necessary to devote so much time to ceremony and that there was no need to fatten up these particular people for the gallows.

On the 19th of December one of our guards told us that Cardinal and Dequette had been notified to prepare themselves to mount the scaffold within the next two days. That aroused in us the hope that the others at least would meet a better fate,

It was on the 21st December, at nine o'clock in the morning that our two unfortunate comrades mounted the scaffold, erected above the door of the wall surrounding the Montreal gaol; they were supported by Father Labelle, then parish priest of Chateauguay, their confessor. Some hours after the execution, Father Labelle came to see us and described to us the terrible circumstances associated with this scene. Poor young Duquette (he was only twenty-two years of age) endured terrible suffering; the executioner had to hang him twice, the rope in the first instance, being badly adjusted and becoming tangled in falling, he had smashed his head against the edge of the scaffold so that it became covered with blood.

This day was one of profound distress for all of us, but we were almost certain of the eternal salvation of our friends, and we passed in prayers a part of those long hours of the day of our brothers' execution. We expected, or at any rate, some of us did, a similar fate; for the political trials followed one another without interruption, before the Court Martial, in spite of the generous as well as skilful protests of the counsel for the accused, Messrs. Drummond[2] and Hart, who did not cease to protest against the incompetence of the tribunal and the illegality of the proceedings. We know that the twelve executions which took place, in the light of the condemnations made by this exceptional and arbitrarily established tribunal, have been described as judicial murders by distinguished jurists of the English parliament.

One should not be surprised at failing to see French-Canadian names added to those of our defending counsel before the Court Martial. The reason for this is that the term "Canadian" was of itself suspect in the eyes of the authorities of the day. Compatriots would have done us more harm than good from the fact of their origin alone. Proof of that could be found in the way in which Messrs. Féréole Pelletier and R. A. R. Hubert were received by some members of the Court which tried us, in an attempt to intervene in favour of the accused. I was told that in reply one of them used these words: "Rebels defending rebels."

When, in passing, I say a word or two about the competence of the Court before which we were summoned to appear, I do not wish it to be understood that I find anything extraordinary in our being brought to trial or even to raise my voice against the sentences in so far as they are bound up with the facts; but I mean that the rights guaranteed by those same laws which we were accused of having wished to upset were then violated. Besides, it is an almost inevitable result of any revolution, and, as far as I am concerned, by admitting the act, I have accepted all its consequences; this, however, did not deprive me of the right of making use, in the defence of my life, of all the legal exceptions and all the facts which weighed in my favour.

On the 8th of January, 1839, I received the order to hold myself in readiness to appear before the Court Martial; eleven of my companions in captivity also received the same instruction. On the 9th of January we were taken, in chains, in a Black Maria to the Pied-du-Courant Gaol. When passing through the walls surrounding this gaol we walked under the scaffold, all freshly spattered with the blood of our friends Cardinal and Duquette.

Some hours after our arrival at this place, Messrs. Drummond and Hart paid us a visit in our cells to ask us for the information which they needed for our defence.

From time to time, during our incarceration, certain legal functionaries of that period had subjected us to interrogations in which they tried to obtain information against the principal leaders of the Canadian faction concerning whom there existed no evidence of any flagrant guilt in the taking up of arms. I mention this matter to show the whole horror of our situation. Besides, one knows that, on occasions such as these, there does not lack men whose zeal often exceeds the scope of the powers that they employ; it is not then astonishing that we met some of these men on the painful road that we were again following. On the other hand, it is as just as it is consoling to say that several officers of the army and some civil servants exhibited in regard to us, feelings which honour them and have behaved towards us as good hearts and honest minds always can when considering those whom misfortune has smitten.

That reminds me that I must not forget to place on record here the noble generosity of the clergy and the residents of Montreal, who, during the course of this dreary and severe winter, did not allow a day to pass without bringing relief and consolation to the political prisoners collected by the hundred within the precincts of the city. Several Canadian ladies, amongst others Mesdames Gauvin and Gamelin,[3] have given proof of a charity and a devotion which neither cold, nor fatigue, nor opposition nor hindrance could shake. I wish that I were able here to thank them worthily as much in my own name as in the names of my comrades, but words are powerless in such a situation. To God alone is reserved the power of rewarding such deeds; these noble women have become Sisters of Charity; they will go and join, in the joy that knows no anguish, the choirs that in heaven are composed of the saintly daughters of Catholic charity.

5

The Trial

We were arraigned for the first time before the Court-Martial on the 11th of January; as I have already said, we numbered twelve, including myself. Here are the names of my fellow-accused: Dr. Perrigo, J. Bte, Henri Brien, Chevalier de Lorimier, Joseph Dumouchel, Louis Dumouchel, Ignace Gabriel Chevrefils, Jacques Goyette, Toussaint Rochon, Joseph Wattier, Jean Laberge and F. X. Touchette.

Immediately following our appearance before our judges, Major-General Clitherow, President of the Court, composed of fifteen army officers, sent us into an anteroom of the Court-house, (This Court-martial held its sittings in the old Palais de Justice) where we remained for ten minutes or so, at the expiration of which we were brought back into the room where the Court was sitting, all of us, with the exception of Dr. Perrigo, who has never undergone trial. In explanation of this extraordinary exception, the Doctor informed us that he owed this favour to his title of Freemason. I sincerely hope, as far as I myself am concerned, never to receive any favour as a member of a Society forbidden by the church ... Freemasonry, or something as little worthy of commendation, had then reduced our number to eleven. Dr. Perrigo was not a Frenchman by birth.

The proceedings took place in English, a language that the majority of us understood not at all, or only slightly; but our counsel, Messrs. Drummond and Hart, were indefatigable and kept us well-informed of all that was happening in connection with ourselves, and as it were without our knowledge. May these gentlemen please accept here, the expression, somewhat weak, perhaps, but nevertheless heartfelt, of my gratitude.

Every morning at nine o'clock we were brought to the Palais de Justice in the same vehicle which had conveyed us from La Pointe-à-Callière to the gaol, escorted by a squad of mounted volunteers.

On the 18th of January occurred the execution of five others of our compatriots whose trial had preceded ours, Théophile Decoigne, Joseph Robert, Ambrose Sanguinette, Charles Sanguinette and F. X. Hamelin. The execution took place at nine o'clock, and, on this particular day, the hour for our visit to the Court was postponed. At a quarter to ten we set out ... Near the door of the jail we saw the five corpses of our friends stretched out on the snow in their convict uniforms.

It would seem that scenes like these should be sufficient to satisfy the fury and hatred with which a certain section of the populace was at that time animated; not at all! A volunteer told us, pointing out to us with his finger these corpses, the sight of which wrung our very hearts, that soon we would be in the same position; and that very same day, our vehicle, on its passage, stirred up the same threats, the same insults, the same outcries as on the other days.

Our trial was marked by an accident which happened to one of our judges, whose name I prefer to suppress. He had had his lower jaw broken by a blow given by a Canadian from the suburb of Saint Joseph during a quarrel of which a dog fight, so it seemed, had been the cause or the pretext. We saw him afterwards upon the bench, his face covered with bandages.

The ludicrous became mingled with the tragic in order to overwhelm us with every kind of suffering and humiliation; but a feeling more powerful than all our sufferings sustained us - the religious feeling; religion had kept up the courage of those of our friends put to death, it had inspired them to pardon the insults, and revealed the open sky above the scaffold; religion also sustained us during those terrible days. The members of the clergy paid us very frequent visits. The Bishop of Montreal, at that time Monsignor Lartigue, and his coadjutor, Monsignor Bourget, brought us spiritual consolation. The Abbots Truteau and Lavoie from the Bishop's Palace, our Confessors, came every other day to prepare us for death. If these lines should ever reach these worthy ministers of the church, I hope they will do me the favour of accepting the thanks that I offer them from the depths of my soul, and that they will be good enough, each one of them, to offer to God some prayers so that the good-feelings with which they inspired me in view of the death on the gibbet from which I escaped, may accompany me in face of that death, whatever it may prove to be, which will make me pay the tribute to nature, resulting from the fall of man.

During my trial, my parents came from St. Polycarpe to pay me a visit. When they arrived at Montreal at the hour when we were facing our judges, my father and mother had taken their place at the foot of the outer staircase of the Palais-de-Justice. At the moment when, hand-cuffed together, two by two, and led between two rows of soldiers, we were making our way back to the gaol, at the conclusion of the hearing, my gaze met those of the authors of my being. This happened at the foot of the stairway. Scarcely were we seen and recognised than my mother, quick as a flash, letting go my father's arm, rushed towards me, crying, "Ah! this poor child!" And, as these words and the sight of this maternal outburst penetrated my whole being, I saw the soldiers thrust aside my mother whom my father had followed, so as to lead her far from the place where this scene occurred. Still this remains today the most vivid in my imagination of all those of which I have been the author, or of which I have been the witness, during the course of those events so full of tragic incidents.

"Oh, Holy Mary, mother of sorrows and of the unhappy ones of this world," I exclaimed to myself, stepping up into the Black Maria, "pray for my poor mother."

Two hours later, my good parents came into the gaol and embraced me ... Twice, almost in succession, my mother fainted in my arms; twice I felt her heart-beats cease when pressed close to mine, beating as though it would break. At this moment I suffered the greatest anguish it has been my lot to endure during the course of a life which has suffered so much.

Following an adjournment of two days, our trial was continued and completed on the 21st January. Eight times we had been dragged, hand-cuffed, before the special court which was to decide our lives. During these long days of our trial, the abuse and insults levelled at us did not diminish on the part of the rabble which crowded round us on our passage, and invaded the approaches to the Court. Some of our judges even did not spare us gross insults; some of them also amused themselves, during the sittings sketching little figures hanging from gibbets and these coarse caricatures which they passed to one another before our gaze, appeared to amuse them greatly . . . May these jests weigh heavily on their consciences.

In justice and in gratitude, I must say that, as far as I, myself, am concerned, the witnesses for the Crown showed much sympathy for me and did not forget to testify concerning anything which might exonerate me or weigh in my favour. I enter these details because it is history, and because in all this there is a profound lesson for everyone.

On the 24th of January, about three o'clock in the afternoon, one after the other we were made to pass into the office of the gaoler, where the three judge advocates of the Court-Martial, Messrs. Dominique Mondelet and C. D. Day, and Captain Miller pronounced sentence on us .... We were, all eleven of us, condemned to be hanged![4]

We expected this decision; but a sentence like this never fails, on that account, to produce a profound impression; then, too, the majority of my companions were fathers of families whose wives and children were already homeless, as a result of the destruction of their property by fire. For myself, I saw my mother succumbing under the weight of her grief.

Very soon afterwards we were placed in locked cells, two by two, and close to other prisoners similarly condemned to death, there to await the day of execution, which was not finally fixed. Scarcely had the judges left us than the two charitable priests of whom I have already spoken, Fathers Truteau and Lavoie, having learnt the news of our sentences, were with us; they remained within the gaol until eight o'clock in the evening, engaged in their ministry of salvation.

6

The Condemned

We were, then, in cells, two by two; we remained thus separated for several days, during which an excellent man of the name of Lesiége, himself a political accused, though but little involved, came and cooked our food in the passage-way which separated our cells, and in which he had his quarters. Soon we were permitted to meet together in this passage-way from ten o'clock in the morning until four o'clock in the afternoon. As can be imagined, this was a great consolation to us and something necessary for our health.

We did not cherish any great hope of a reprieve; the scenes which we had witnessed were of such a character as to make us abandon all hope; but what position, however desperate it may be, can entirely remove hope or fantasy from the heart of man?

In accordance with what our Counsel had managed to learn, although we were all grouped together under the same sentence of death, we were graded in the judge's notes in the following order of culpability: 1st, De Lorimier ; 2nd, J. B. Brien; 3rd, Joseph Dumouchel; 4th, Toussaint Rochon; 5th, F. X. Prieur; 6th, Jos. Wattier; 7th, Jean Laberge; 8th, Gabriel Chèvrefils ; 9th Jacques Goyette; 10th, Louis Dumouchel; 11th; F. X. Touchette.

During the course of our trial, one of my generous defending-counsel, Mr. Hart, told me that he had it on good authority that some disinterested persons had presented a petition to His Excellency the Administrator, Sir John Colborne, recommending me personally to the Royal clemency, in whose powers it lay, as the King's representative.

This request was due, I was informed, to the efforts and the entreaties of the excellent ladies of the Ellice family, who in this wise, wished to recognise the kindnesses which I had shown them formerly, when in command of the troops in the village of Beauharnais.

My father and my mother came again to see me during the first days of February. After the moments devoted to the outpourings of our natural feelings, I spoke to my parents of my death, telling them they must be prepared for the worst. I wished to spare them, should my execution take place, the terrible scenes which precede the mounting of the scaffold, and I told them that I would like to take my last farewell of them on the evening before the day appointed. I informed them that the authorities handed over to their families the bodies of the executed, and I begged them to have the goodness to deposit my remains in the cemetery of the parish where I was born, in the shade of the church where the baptismal ceremony had made me a Christian, and where I had taken my first Communion. To these words addressed to my worthy parents, my mother replied in a voice full of confidence, that I would not die upon the gallows. "Let us pray to the Holy Virgin, she will save you," she said to me ... A few minutes later the tears and embraces of all three of us terminated this visit.

Of how many scenes of this kind and much more heart-rending still have not these walls of the Pied-du-Courant Gaol been the witnesses! All my companions in captivity and under sentence of death were fathers of families, with the exception of two. The women and the children came to see those whose love and affection, in all probability, the hand of the hangman was soon about to snatch away. All that was taking place beneath our very eyes; our griefs as well as our condemnation, were shared in common amongst us. Of all the poor wives of the condemned, Mrs. De Lorimier is the one who excited the most pity. It seemed like foreboding; and, besides this poor family, when losing its head, was losing all its means of supporting existence. Our unfortunate friend spoke continually to his wife about his poverty; he sought to find some way of suggesting to her ways and means of bringing up his children, and when he realized the impossibility of finding such means within the bounds of possibility, he always ended by telling her, "Dame Providence will not forsake you."

On the 12th of February, two of the gentlemen from the Seminary of Saint Sulpice paid us a visit at about eight o'clock in the evening. They came at this late hour to inform us of the news that they had learnt, viz: that the authorities had placed an order for seven coffins. They came, therefore, especially to exhort us to offer gladly to God the sacrifice of a mortal existence so that we might obtain the favour of an everlasting life of happiness. These worthy gentlemen remained an hour in the gaol, conversing on heavenly things and praying at intervals; then they took leave of us after bestowing their blessing.

We were then quite convinced that the first men whose names were on the list which I gave previously were to be executed, and I was one of the number. I believe I can say that this prospect found me calm and resigned to my fate: when taking up arms in the month of November, I was under no illusions regarding the dangers of all sorts to which I was exposing myself, and, next, I had familiarized myself with the idea of death upon the gallows to the extent that the question, as far as I was concerned, was no more than one of time.

In the silence of my cell, and of the night, after the departure of the good priests, I communed with my God for some hours; then I lay down, and until morning slept a deep and restful sleep; for the face of death for a Christian is not wholly sadness and terror. How can it be otherwise for him who nourishes his mind and soul on those splendid promises made to those whose faith permits them to say: "I have put my faith in Thee, O Lord, and I will never be confounded." Such were my thoughts, and I am sure those of my comrades also, resting safely within the arms of the Church which was preparing us for the passage from a life of misery to a glorious one through the care of its ministers.

The communication which had been made to us in the evening by the good priests had been to each one individually and within our cells; the hour when we assembled in the corridor, our meeting was a most affecting one; those who believed they were not now to face the gallows showed themselves more distressed than those of us who expected soon to die. Had it not been for the thought of the beloved ones whom those condemned were leaving on earth, I am quite certain that we would have experienced a veritable serene joy at thus feeling ourselves on the edge of the tomb and on the threshold of eternity.

Friends came to visit us and to tell us it was rumoured that the executions were to take place the following Friday morning; it was then Wednesday; but we had not received any official notification of any sort concerning our fate. We were one and all condemned to death; the moments of our existence were at the will and pleasure of Sir John Colborne : that was all we knew.

At three o'clock in the afternoon the turnkey came and told us that the three Judge Advocates had just gone into the gaoler's office; they were coming to notify the victims intended for the scaffold that the day of their execution was fixed for the following Friday. *It was little more than one day's notice!*

A few minutes later, the door of our prison opened, and the gaoler, stopping in the doorway opened by his assistant, called out: "Charles Hindenlang!" The latter, answering the call, left the room, of which the door was closed again upon us. Charles Hindenlang was a young French Protestant, who, having seen military service in the United States where he had resided temporarily, had joined up enthusiastically with the insurrectionary movement in Lower Canada.

About ten minutes later, the door opened again, and the gaoler called, "Chevalier de Lorimier!" The latter departed with the warders, and the door closed a second time.

A third time the door opened: I was busy at the back of the room, cooking something in a saucepan, when I heard myself called. Leaving my cooking pot where it was, I walked towards the gaoler, saying to my comrades, "It's my turn now!" but the gaoler said to me in English, "It's not you that I called; it's Mr. Lepailleur, and it's to give him some food that his parents have sent him."

Our two companions, De Lorimier and Hindenlang, returned to us very soon afterwards, and told us gathered together in an excited group that had been formed to receive them: "Good news for you; we are the only two victims selected in this section, but there are three others taken from the other parts of the gaol, and they are, Rémi Narbonne, Francois Nicolas and Amable Daunais."

There were at that very moment with us two ladies, relatives of the unhappy De Lorimier, his sister and his cousin, accompanied by a gentleman friend of the family. These poor ladies burst into tears. The victim consoled them with holy words, full of faith and resignation. "My sacrifice is made," he said; "and I cherish the hope of going to see my God; one thing alone will cast a gloom over my last moments, and that is the thought of the destitution of my wife and my little children; but I commit them to the care of Divine Providence."

Poor Hindenlang, in whom his religion did not inspire the same feelings as did that of Lorimier, was far from exhibiting, in his words and behaviour, as worthy and as cheerful a demeanour. It was easy to see that the thought of a future life was disturbing his soul; not knowing what to cling to in order, without faintheartedness, to face up to this immense prospect, he appealed for it only to his personal courage, which, undoubtedly, was very great. Nevertheless, it was easy to see that this support was only a fragile reed. In order to divert his thoughts and to put a brave aspect on his countenance, he assumed an attitude of stoical indifference, and now and again, a kind of foolish gaiety scarcely suitable in such circumstances.

How we pitied him, seeing him thus on his way towards a future, which, happy or unhappy, was doomed never to come to an end. For a moment we had cherished the hope of seeing him enter into the bosom of the Church, bearing away with him the pardon of those whose mission it is to bind and unbind, both on earth and for heaven; our hope proved false. He was content to admire the effect produced by the Catholic religion upon his companions in misfortune; but to imitate them he was lacking in that moral courage which would have allowed him to follow their example.

About six o'clock in the evening the turnkeys came and told us that we must go back into our cells; our visitors then withdrew, grief-stricken. I have already said that we were two to a cell. Until this time the cell companion of De Lorimier had been Dr. Brien. Now the latter came and asked me to be good enough to exchange cells with him, saying that he did not feel that he had the strength to share the cell with the victim.

Ah! Thus it is, you see; remorse was gnawing at the conscience of this wretched fellow who had obtained a semi-pardon bought at the shameful cost of turning informer as we discovered later. One can imagine, then, what sort of feelings proximity to such a man would arouse in the mind of one whom he had betrayed, this man who was about to die in the heart of honour and the peace of God.

I became then the cell-companion of Chevalier de Lorimier. In the evening his confessor came to see him, and remained alone with him for a whole hour, during which I withdrew into the passage-way. At the end of this sacred intercourse between the repentant sinner and the bearer of pardon for sins, De Lorimier was calm; his face seemed even to manifest a suspicion of mirth. We were again locked up together: I prayed with him during a part of the night, then we slept peacefully one beside the other.

In the morning, quiet and rested, he prayed for a long time, then he spoke to me at length about his wife and children; he confided them to the care of Providence. With difficulty I was able to reply to words so appealingly, so resigned, so Christian, so greatly did my feelings overcome me.

When the cell doors were opened in the morning at the usual hour of ten o'clock, all eyes were turned, with mingled interest and sadness, towards the two victims, whom young William Lévêque, cell-companion of Hindenlang and myself, companion of Lorimier, led by the arm towards the tactfully formed groups of our unhappy comrades. De Lorimier was resigned and dignified. Hindenlang courageous and noisy. I prepared something for our breakfast; but De Lorimier ate little. He walked with measured step up and down the passageway and spoke often of his wife, who was to visit him in the afternoon. He dreaded this interview for his unfortunate better half.

About three o'clock in the afternoon, Mrs. Lorimier, accompanied by the sister and the cousin of her husband, and escorted by a Mr. de Lorimier, a cousin of the condemned man, came into our quarters. On her face Mrs. de Lorimier carried an expression of grief that was heart-breaking, but she did not weep; her two companions both burst into tears.

We had made arrangements to give a farewell dinner to our two unfortunate friends. The table, loaded with eatables prepared, by our instruction, by the gaoler, had been placed in a room situated near the door opening on to the passage-way. At four o-clock we sat down to table, with Hindenlang presiding at the repast. De Lorimier did not occupy the seat reserved for him; but he came and took a glass of wine with us. During the meal, he walked up and down the corridor, with Mrs. Lorimier on his arm. The other members of his family occupied seats, sometimes within the cells, or again in the passage-way. The ladies, from time to time, lavished soothing caresses on the poor unfortunate wife.

Over our table prevailed a kind of forced gaiety, which Hindenlang, on his part, made somewhat noisy. During these happier moments the prison authorities permitted the admission of six inquisitive persons, amongst whom, I was told, was the editor of *The Herald* newspaper. They stood within, near the door, visibly astonished at the character of this scene. After having had pointed out to them those who the following day were to ascend the scaffold, they withdrew without uttering a word.

A moment later we were told that Mme. de Lorimier had fainted.

She was lying at this time in a completely unconscious state in her husband's cell.

Just as evening was approaching, Mr. de Lorimier's confessor came and spent some time alone with him in his cell; then he said "Courage" to the two victims, offered some words of Christian consolation to Mme. de Lorimier and took leave of all of us.

The two men condemned to death, Mr. Leveque and myself had been allowed to remain outside our cells much longer than usual; at ten o'clock the gaoler came and told us that we must return there. This was the time that the unfortunate de Lorimier dreaded most, and that we also saw approaching with a pang of grief at our heart. Some relatives and friends had come to join the three members of the family who accompanied Mme. Lorimier and who were to undertake the painful but charitable task of taking her back to the township.

The poor young woman was then about to bid an eternal farewell to her husband. After many falterings, sobs and tears, she threw her arms round his neck and again fainted. De Lorimier raised her in his arms, and, holding her like a child that is being put into its cradle, moved towards the door, his eyes fixed on the agonised face of his life's companion. When he reached the thresh-hold he kissed his wife's colourless brow and placed her in the arms of her relatives, recommending them to take every possible care of her ... and the door closed again upon us.

On regaining our cell door, de Lorimier said to me: "The worst blow is given!" He was composed, but pale as death.

He passed part of the night in prayers, and in writing a letter which was a kind of political testament, [5] then, acting on the advice that had been given to him, he went to bed. I watched over him; he slept very quietly for nearly three hours.

About seven o'clock (Friday, 15th of February, 1839) his Confessor arrived; he came to bring him the last Sacrament, and was to wait so as to accompany him to the scaffold. The condemned man received the Holy Communion with fervency in his cell, where he remained until after eight o'clock in a pious attitude with his confessor. The time having come for de Lorimier to prepare himself for the death march, the priest withdrew for some little time; it was I who assisted my unhappy companion to make his sacrificial toilet. As I was fixing a little white necktie round his neck he said to me, "Leave the space necessary for placing the rope." Tears poured in streams from my eyes, when I received from him such an injunction.

As soon as his toilet was finished, de Lorimier left the cell, and, addressing all the prisoners, asked them to repeat in unison, the morning prayer. He himself did so in a voice loud, strong and well pronounced. At the invitation of de Lorimier, Hindenlang, who thus far had remained in his cell, left it and joined us to take part in the prayer; but he stood all the time upright, with his head bent forward and his hands clasped upon his chest. Oh! how we pitied him then, and how we thanked God for having granted us the grace of belonging to his Holy Church.

At the conclusion of the prayer the two condemned men took a cup of coffee.

I had asked our unfortunate friends to leave me as a souvenir something belonging intimately to each of them. Thereupon each one gave me a lock of his hair. That of de Lorimier was contained in a note of which the following is a copy:-

Montreal Gaol,
15th February, 1839.

Dear Prieur, You ask me for a word by which to remember me; dear friend, what do you wish me to write? I am setting out for the gallows. Be of good courage, and I die your friend.

Good-bye,

CHEVALIER DE LORIMIER.

Hindenlang had written, during the morning, a few lines of which he left us a copy; it was the address which he felt he ought to deliver to those who were witnesses of his execution. [6]

This statement was a true exemplification of his nature, generous but fanatical, and was the result of that revolutionary education which was still current in France, and which was spreading through Canada. The unhappy young man got it into his head (as did all of us, or nearly all, victims of taking up arms) that Canada was in a state fit for conquest and for maintaining its independence. 1 do not really understand today how such an idea had been able to take such strong roots in the heart of our populace, and to persist amongst us political convicts, considering our speedy dispersal and the disasters which followed in its train.

At about a quarter to nine o'clock, the gaoler, accompanied by some military officers, several soldiers and a fair number of inquisitive persons, came looking for the two victims. De Lorimier, on seeing the procession approaching, said to the gaoler in a firm voice, "I am ready." He embraced me, saluted all his friends, to whom he had already said good-bye, and left with his companion, Hindenlang.

I have mentioned that their three companions for the gallows were lodged in another part of the gaol, so that I was not able to have any association with them.

The good priest who attended De Lorimier had recommended us to pray during the execution, which we did with all the fervour of which we were capable. Religion is always very real for people whose hearts are good and spirits true. But it is especially in face of death that this quality of truth shines with all its brilliance.

Three quarters of an hour after the departure of our unfortunate comrades, an employee of the prison, a Canadian, came into our quarters; he told us, in a flood of tears, that the five victims were in the next world.

These executions were the last; twelve political prisoners had reddened the gallows with their blood between the 21st December, 1838 and the 15th February, 1839, namely, Messrs. Cardinal, Duquette, Decoigne, Robert, Ambroise Sanguinette, Charles Sanguinette, Hamelin, de Lorimier, Hindenlang, Narbonne, Nicolas and Daunais.

But if the executions then ceased, thanks, we were told, to formal instructions received from England, political trials and sentences of death did not.

Some time elapsed without our hearing any news of our future fate. When I speak of news, I mean official news; for the government only expressed its decision regarding us, transportation or the gallows, a few hours in advance.

In the month of June we were informed that there was a rumour that those condemned to death had; or were going to have, their sentences commuted to transportation for life. As for myself, I was resigned to anything. We had become also habituated to disaster, and we could hardly be in a worse state than we were, as we then believed ... We were wrong.

We continued then to occupy the Montreal gaol, receiving from the government only bread and water, but generously helped by our compatriots, and shut up every day in our cells from four o'clock in the afternoon until ten o'clock the following morning.

My good old parents came to see me several times during the period of my detention. My poor mother, although much distressed, was less affected by the prospect of my exile than by that of my death. She said, "You will come back home again."

7

States of Suspense

Before continuing the story of my adventures, and of those of my friends and companions in misfortune, I think I should give the following list, drawn up by me at the time, and which provides the information which the reader will not peruse without interest concerning the persons condemned by the Court Martial of 1838.

It is not without importance to remark that, in addition to imprisonment, trial and condemnation, the greater part of the victims of this unhappy period saw all their possessions reduced to ashes, before the day of their execution, or of their departure for exile. It is these useless and inhuman burnings of hundreds of dwellings which have given to Sir John Colborne the nickname of "The Old Firebrand."

So as not to make the following list needlessly overlong, I shall make use of some abbreviations; thus I shall say simply "burnt" to describe those whose property has been destroyed by fire; I shall say "transported" to distinguish those whose death sentence has been changed to transportation for life in the Australian penal colony; "exiled" to indicate those who have been instructed to leave the country. I shall adopt the order set down in the table of proceedings as carried out before the Court-Martial.

First Trial

Commenced the 28th November, ended the 14th December, 1838.

Joseph Narcisse Cardinal, lawyer, of the Parish of Chateauguay, aged 30 years, father of five children, burnt, condemned to death and executed 21st December, 1838.

Joseph Duquette, law student, of the Parish of Chateauguay, aged 22 years, unmarried, burnt, condemned to death and executed, 21st December.

Joseph L'Ecuyer, farmer, of Chateauguay, aged 30 years, father of one child, burnt, condemned to death, released on bail.

Jean Louis Thibert, farmer, of Chateauguay, aged 52 years, father of three children, condemned to death, transported.

Jean Marie Thibert, farmer, of Chateauguay, aged 37 years, father of four children, condemned to death, transported.

Leandre Ducharme, Commercial Traveller, of Montreal, unmarried, aged 22 years, condemned to death, transported.

Joseph Guimond, farmer, of Chateauguay, aged 50 years, father of three children, condemned to death, transported.

Louis Guerin, farmer, of Chateauguay, aged 36 years, father of four children, condemned to death, transported.

Edouard Thérien, of Chateauguay, acquitted.

Antoine Côte, farmer, of Chateauguay, aged 48 years, father of eight children, liberated under police superintendence.

François Maurice Lepailleur, Sheriff's Officer, of Chateauguay, aged 32 years, father of two children, burnt, condemned to death, transported.

Louis Lesiège, shoemaker, of Chateauguay, acquitted.

Second Trial

Commenced the 17th December, ended the 22nd December, 1838

Charles Huot, lawyer de Napierville, aged 52 years, unmarried, condemned to death, transported.

Third Trial

Commenced the 24th December, ended the 2nd January, 1839.

Guillaume Lévesque, law student, of Montreal, aged 19 years, unmarried, condemned to death, exiled.

Pierre Théophile Decoigne, lawyer, of Napierville, aged 27 years, father of two children, burnt, condemned to death, executed 18th January, 1839.

Achille Morin, farmer, of Napierville, aged 22 years, unmarried, condemned to death, transported.

Joseph Jacques Hébert, farmer, of Napierville, aged 38 years, unmarried, condemned to death, transported.

Hubert Drossin Leblanc, farmer, of Napierville, aged 31 years, father of four children, burnt, condemned to death, transported.

Francois Trépanier, Junior agriculturist, of Napierville, aged 16 years, condemned to death, released on bail.

Pierre Hector Morin, Master of a ship, of Napierville, aged 58 years, father of five children, burnt, condemned to death, transported.

Joseph Paré, farmer, of Napierville, aged 45 years, married, no children, burnt, condemned to death, transported.

Louis Lemelin, farmer, of Napierville, acquitted.

J. Bte. Dozois, farmer, of Napierville, acquitted.

Fourth Trial

Commenced 3rd January and ended 10th January, 1839.

Joseph Robert, farmer, of Saint Philippe, aged 59, father of five children, condemned to death and executed 18th January, 1839.

Jacques Robert, farmer, of Saint Edouard, acquitted.

Ambroise Sanguinette, farmer of Saint Constant, aged 38 years, father of five children, condemned to death and executed 18th January.

Charles Sanguinette, farmer, of Saint Philippe, aged 36 years, father of two children, condemned to death and executed 18th January.

Paschal Pinsonneault, tanner, of Saint Philippe, aged 28 years, unmarried, condemned to death, transported.

Francois Xavier Hamelin, farmer, of Saint Philippe, aged 23 years, unmarried, condemned to death and executed 18th January.

Theophile Robert, farmer, of Saint Edouard, aged 24 years, without children, condemned to death, transported.

Joseph Longtin, of Saint Constant, acquitted.

Jacques Longtin, farmer, of Saint Constant, aged 59 years, father of eleven children, condemned to death, transported.

Jacques Robert, of Saint Edouard, acquitted.

Fifth Trial

Commenced 11th January, ended 21st January, 1839.

Jean Baptiste Henri Brien, medical practitioner, of Sainte Martine, aged 23 years, unmarried, condemned to death, exiled.

Ignace Gabriel Chevrefils,[7] farmer, of Saint Martine, aged 43 years, father of seven children, condemned to death, transported.

Joseph Dumouchelle, farmer, of Saint Martine, aged 45 years, father of four children, burnt, condemned to death, transported.

Louis Dumouchelle,[7] innkeeper, of Saint Martine, aged 40 years, father of six children, burnt, condemned to death, transported.

Jacques Goyette, farmer, of Saint Clement de Beauharnais, aged 48 years, father of three children, burnt, condemned to death, transported.

Toussaint Rochon, wheelwright, of Saint Clement, aged. 28 years, father of two children, burnt, condemned to death, transported.

Francois Xavier Prieur, merchant, of Saint Timothee, aged 23 years, bachelor, burnt, condemned to death, transported.

Joseph Wattier dit Lanoie, trader, of The Cedars, aged 57 years, father of nine children, burnt, condemned to death, released on bail.

Chevalier de Lorimier, lawyer, of Montreal, aged 34 years, father of three children, condemned to death and executed 15th February, 1839.

Jean Laberge, carpenter, of Sainte Martine, aged 34 years, father of six children, burnt, condemned to death, transported.

Francois Xavier Touchette, blacksmith, of Sainte Martine, aged 30 years, father of four children, burnt, condemned to death, transported.

Sixth Trial

Commenced 26th January, ended 6th February, 1839.

Charles Hindenlang, Soldier, of Paris, France, aged 29 years, unmarried, condemned to death and executed 15th February, 1839.

Seventh Trial

Commenced 26th January, ended 6th February, 1839.

Pierre Rémi Narbonne, Sheriff's Officer, aged 36 years, father of two children, condemned to death and executed 15th February, 1839.

Amable Daunais, farmer, of Saint Cyprien, aged 21 years, unmarried, condemned to death and executed 15th February.

Constant Bousquet, farmer, of Saint Cyprien, case dismissed.

Pierre Lavoie, farmer, of Saint Cyprien, aged 48 years, father of nine children, condemned to death, transported.

Antoine Doré, shop-keeper, of Saint Jacques the Less, acquitted.

Antoine Coupal, alias *Lareine,* farmer, of Sainte Marguerite, aged 49 years, father of twelve children, condemned to death, transported.

Theodore Bédard, farmer, of Sainte Marguerite, aged 47 years, father of ten children, condemned to death, transported.

Francois Camyré, in keeper, of Saint Constant, father of five children, burnt, condemned to death, released on bail.

Francois Bigonesse alias *Beaucaire,* farmer, of Saint Cyprien, aged 47 years, father of seven children, condemned to death, transported.

Joseph Marceau, farmer, of Saint Cyprien, aged 30 years, father of two children, condemned to death, transported.

Francois Nicolas, Schoolmaster, of Saint Athanese, aged 44 years, unmarried, condemned to death and executed 15th February, 1839.

Eighth Trial

Commenced 7th February, ended 21st February, 1839.

James Perrigo, salesman, of Ste. Martine, acquitted.

Louis Turcot, farmer, of Sainte Martine, aged 33 years, father of six children, condemned to death, transported.

Jean Marie Lefèvre, of Sainte Martine, case dismissed.

Godfrey Chaloux, of Sainte Martine, case dismissed.

Desire Bourbonnais, blacksmith, of Saint Clement, aged 19 years, unmarried, condemned to death, transported.

Michel Longtin, farmer, of Saint Clement, aged 53 years, father of five children, condemned to death, transported.

Charles Roy, alias *Lapensee,* Senior, farmer, of Saint Clement, aged 50 years, father of one child, burnt, condemned to death, transported.

Francois Xavier Provost, innkeeper, of Saint Clement, father of three children, burnt, condemned to death, transported.

Isidore Tremblay, farmer, of Saint Clement, acquitted.

Andre Papineau, alias *Montigny,* blacksmith, of Saint Clement, aged 30 years, father of *seven* children, condemned to death, transported.

David Gagnon, carpenter, of St. Timothee, aged 30 years, father of two children, condemned to death, transported.

Charles Papin, bailiff and hotelkeeper, of Saint Timothee, aged 29 years, father of three children, burnt, condemned to death, released on bail.

Ninth Trial

Commenced 22nd February, ended 28th February, 1839.

Louis Bourdon, merchant, of Saint Cesaire, aged 22 years, father of *two* children, condemned to death, transported.

J. Bte. Bousquet, miller, of Saint Cesaire, aged 39 years, unmarried, condemned to death, transported.

Francois Guertin, farmer, of Saint Cesaire, aged 43 years, unmarried, condemned to death, transported.

Tenth Trial

Commenced 1st March, ended 11th March, 1839.

Charles Guillaume Bouc, citizen, of Terrebonne, aged 46 years, father of seven children, condemned to death, transported.

Leon Leclerc, farmer of Terrebonne, aged 40 years, father of six children, condemned to death, released on bail.

Paul Gravel, farmer, of Terrebonne, aged 23 years, unmarried, condemned to death, released on bail.

Antoine Roussin, farmer, of Terrebonne, aged 36 years, father of five children, condemned to death, released on bail.

Francois St. Louis, farmer, of Terrebonne, aged 36 years, father of four children, condemned to death, released on bail.

Edouard Paschal Rochon, wheelwright, of Terrebonne, aged 38 years, father of one child, condemned to death, transported.

Eleventh Trial

Commence 12th March, ended 19th March, 1839.

Louis Desjayettes, farmer, of Saint Cyprien, aged 38 years, father of two children, burnt, condemned to death, transported.

Jacques David Hébert, farmer, of Saint Cyprien, aged 47 years, father of eight children, burnt, condemned to death, transported.

David Demas, farmer, of Saint Cyprien, aged 26 years, father of four children, condemned to death, released on bail.

Thomas Surprenant, alias Lafontaine, farmer, of Saint Philippe, aged 47 years, father of eleven children, condemned to death, released on bail.

Francois Surprenant, farmer, of Saint Philippe, aged 50 years, father of eleven children, burnt, condemned to death, released on bail.

Hypolite Lanctot, lawyer, of Saint Rerni, aged 23 years, father of two children, condemned to death, transported.

Louis Pinsonnault, farmer, of Saint Rerni, aged 40 years, father of three children, burnt, condemned to death, transported.

Rene Pinsonnault, farmer, of Saint Constant, aged 49 years, father of six children, condemned to death, transported.

Etienne Languedoc, farmer, of Saint Constant, aged 21 years, unmarried, condemned to death, transported.

Benoni Verdon, farmer, of Saint Edouard, aged 30 years, father of five children, burnt, condemned to death, released on bail.

Etienne Langlois, farmer, of Saint Marguerite, aged 25 years, married, without children, condemned to death, transported.

Twelfth Trial

Commenced 20th March, ended 22nd March, 1839.

Charles Mondat, farmer, of Saint Constant, aged 33 years, father of three children, condemned to death, released on bail.

Clovis Patenaude, farmer, of Saint Constant, aged 45 years, father of three children, condemned to death, released on bail.

Moyse Longtin, farmer, of Saint Constant, aged 24 years, unmarried, condemned to death, transported.

Thirteenth Trial

Commenced 25th March, ended 8th April, 1839.

Michel Alarie, carpenter, of Saint Clement, aged 34 years, father of four children, condemned to death, transported.

Joseph Goyette, carpenter, of Saint Clement, aged 28 years, father of two children, condemned to death, transported.

Louis Hénault, lawyer, of Saint Clement, aged 25 years, unmarried, condemned to death, released on bail.

Basile Roy, farmer, of Saint Clement, aged 40 years, father of five children, condemned to death, transported.

Joseph Roy, farmer, of Saint Clement, aged 55 years, father of eight children, condemned to death, released on bail.

Joseph Roy, alias *Lapensee,* son of Louis, farmer, of Saint Clement, aged 24 years, father of one child, condemned to death, transported.

Edouard Tremblay, farmer, of Saint Clement, aged 33 years, unmarried, condemned to death, released on bail.

Philippe Tremblay, farmer, of Saint Clement, aged 26 years, unmarried, condemned to death, released on bail.

Francois Vallée, farmer, of Sainte Martine, aged 30 years, father of three children, burnt, condemned to death, released on bail.

Constant Buisson, blacksmith, of Sainte Martine, aged 28 years, father of one child, condemned to death, transported.

Charles Bergevin, alias *Langevin,* farmer, of Sainte Martine, aged 50 years, father of seven children, burnt, condemned to death, transported.

Antoine Charbonneau, farmer, of Saint Tirnothee, aged 46 years, father of eight children, condemned to death, released on bail.

Joseph Cousineau, farmer, of St. Timothee, aged 40 years, father of five children, condemned to death, released on bail.

Francois Dian, shoemaker, of Saint Tirnothee, aged 48 years, father of six children, condemned to death, released on bail.

Louis Julien, farmer, of Saint Tirnothee, aged 37 years, father of four children, condemned to death, released on bail.

Jean Bte. Trudelle, farmer, of Chateauguay, aged 32 years, father of three children, condemned to death, transported.

Moise Dalton, farmer, of Chateauguay, aged 25 years, father of one child, condemned to death, released on bail.

Samuel Newcombe, doctor of medicine, of Chateauguay, aged 65 years, father of five children, burnt, condemned to death, transported.

Jérémie Rochon, wheelwright, of Saint Vincent de Paul, aged 36 years, father of five children, condemned to death, transported.

Fourteenth Trial

Commenced 10th April, ended 1st May, 1839.

Benjamin Matt, farmer, of Alburgh in the State of Vermont, aged 42 years, father of two children, condemned to death, transported.

This long list takes into account only one part of the sufferings of this year 1838. To gain an idea of the whole, one must remember that certain individuals not included in this list languished for months in the gaols, or for years in lands of exile, that hundreds of families have found themselves out in the street as a result of the burning down of their dwellings.

In all that there is a lesson for all of us, which is so self-evident that there is no necessity to discuss it at length. [8]

Joseph Narcisse Cardinal, executed 1838; and Chevel de Lorimier, executed 1839.

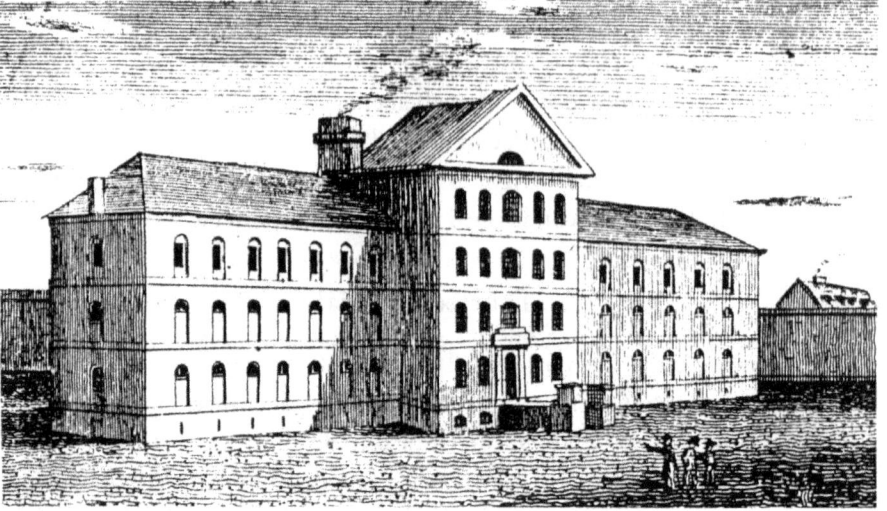

Prison au Pied-du-Courant, Montreal, and the Execution of the "Patriotes", 1839.

8

The Voyage of the Transportees

As the summer began to wear to its close, the report of our departure into exile began to spread, but no one knew what would be the purport of the order of commutation, and complete ignorance prevailed concerning the place where we were to be sent.

At last, after six months of gaol and misery, on the 25th September 1839, at three o'clock in the afternoon, word was sent to fifty-eight of us (see the list in the preceding chapter), all condemned to death, that our sentence had been commuted to one of transportation for life to Australia, and that we should be ready to set out on this voyage of several thousand miles *the next day*. Yes, a notification in the evening for a departure the very next morning, to respectable men, fathers of families, banished for life amidst the convicts in another hemisphere, not for atrocious or dishonorable crimes, but for having given way to the impulses, blameworthy without doubt, but generous, of an ill-directed patriotism.

My only aim, in this brief discussion, is to protest against a spate of articles which have represented the rebels of 1837 and 1838 as monsters, and went even so far as to charge the government of the day with having encouraged revolutions by pardoning the guilty with an excess of softness and clemency. One author, an army officer, said in this connexion, in a work published about Canada and directed against my compatriots, "The loyal Canadians, who had suffered much during the insurrection, were discontented and indignant at this tendency to clemency."[9]

Today, when the passions aroused in those unhappy times have completely subsided, one can, without danger, make allowances for each and everyone, and it should be permitted to those who have suffered so much for their momentary lapse, to prove before going down into the grave, that they should not be confused with the major criminals, and that they have fully paid their debt to the established order of things.

The public had learnt, some hours before we did, that our fate was determined, and the relatives and friends of the condemned had hastened to send- and inform their respective families of their departure, so very soon, for the place of banishment for life.

At eight o'clock in the morning, the day we were due to embark, a great number of parents, wives and children of the convicts invaded the gaol, to say a farewell that was believed to be forever, and which was so for several, the one to a son, the other to a husband, others to a father. All ages were mingled in this reunion of bitter tears and heart-rending cries. The unhappy fathers of families were hardly able to find words of consolation to give to these disconsolate women, to these children left henceforth without any other support than that of the charity of neighbours, friends or the public; they had to content themselves with mingling their tears with those of those creatures so dear to them, and with returning their last fond embraces.

As far as I myself was concerned, I had seen one of my brothers the evening before, and I thanked God for sparing my old parents, who were absent, and especially my mother, the heartbreaking emotions of a scene such as this. I said to myself, when looking at my comrades about to be transported, the greater number of whom were peaceful farmers, "What has anyone to be afraid of now from these fine fellows." If, however, there are any guilty, it is certainly not they!

At eleven o'clock in the morning of the 26th September, a heap of handcuffs was brought into that section of the gaol where I was located. That, added to the noise of opening doors and the clattering of iron that we heard on the neighbouring stairways, made us aware that the hour for departure had arrived.

Very soon all strangers, that is to say, the members of the families of the convicts, were compelled to withdraw, and immediately afterwards, certain civil and military officers proceeded to chain the prisoners together. We were shackled two by two, and led away into the front courtyard of the gaol, between two lines of infantry.

At the door was stationed a detachment of cavalry. There, too, stood wives and children of the convicts, who, warned too late, had not been able to come in time, for one last word with their husbands and fathers in the gaol. Cries, tears, heart-rending farewells passed through the ranks of the soldiers, sometimes a leap towards the convicts, repulsed by the agents of authority.

On leaving the gaol, and finding myself in the open air, I experienced a moment of material well-being impossible to describe: I had not been outside the walls of the gaol since my trial! I inhaled the fresh air in great gulps, and I gazed at the beautiful sky of my native land; but this delight was of short duration, for, very soon recalled to the feeling of reality, I fell into the sad thoughts suggested by the prospect of my unhappy fate.

On leaving our prison quarters, we had been the recipients of expressions of warm sympathy from several of the people employed about the establishment. This does honour to humanity and adds always to the welfare of the prisoners. The medical officer of the gaol, Dr. Arnoldi, who had always acted with much kindness towards us (I speak of M. Arnoldi, Senior, who died at Montreal several years ago) shed warm tears. At the moment when my irons were being put on he grasped my free hand between his own, and pressing me to him affectionately, said, "Courage, my boy!"

There was a crowd in the streets, but the mass of the inquisitive onlookers, it seemed, was stationed at the wharf where the embarkation was to take place, the streets approaching which were filled with people. To distract the crowd, which would possibly have become a source of embarrassment and trouble, we were hastily shepherded, under an escort of cavalry, towards the outlet of the river, where we found the steamer *British America*, which took us on board. We were made to go below the fore-deck, and, a moment later, the vessel left the river at full speed.

In the afternoon our manacles were taken off, and, shortly afterwards, a ration of bread and ham was distributed, which the majority of us scarcely touched, so greatly were they upset by the feelings associated with the departure. There were some of us, as I have mentioned previously, whose homes had been burnt down, and who were leaving behind wives burdened with numerous children, all homeless.

Our boat dropped anchor in Lake St. Pierre. This was, so the crew said, to wait for another vessel, having on board transportees from Upper Canada. The intention was to make only one operation of the tranship-ment of all the prisoners on board the transport which was to convey us all to Australia.

It was about eleven o'clock on 27th September, when in the harbour of Quebec we went alongside the transport vessel, the *Buffalo*. It was a big three-decker ship, equipped, I believe, with fifteen or twenty guns of different sizes, and mounting a crew of about one hundred and fifty men.

Our handcuffs were now put on again and we were immediately placed in the quarters which had been prepared for us, and, good heavens! what quarters they were! They were situated on the third deck, and well below the water-line. There, quite exhausted, in the narrow, gloomy space which, for some months was to be the abode of our sufferings, our fetters were removed and the beds that we were to occupy were distributed amongst us.

So that the intelligent reader may properly understand my descrip-tion, I have had a little diagram prepared, showing the arrangement of these quarters, prepared for one hundred and forty-four prisoners, includ-ing those from Upper as well as Lower Canada, in a between-decks four feet and some inches high, from one deck to the other, by about 75 feet long between two partitions built for the purpose of accommodating us. Each of us enjoyed only the use of a space of about fifty cubic feet, in a place devoid of ventilation, where we passed both our days and our nights, except for the short and infrequent moments when we walked on the main deck.

Our quarters extended then from the third part of the stern of the ship to the space which in merchant vessels is called the store-room. This space, in the centre of the vessel, assumed the shape of a box, 75 feet long, by about 35 feet wide and 4 1/2 feet high, with the exception of a small space at the rear, where a projection of the deck gave an elevation of a little less than six feet, near the hatchway. The centre of this box was, as regards its length, traversed by a row of boxes and packing cases, making a pile at least twelve feet wide, and extending from one deck to the other, sepa-rating the 'tween decks into two distinct compartments, communicating with one another by means of two passage ways left open at each end, which passage ways corresponded with two hatches provided with iron grilles and guarded by sentries.

Explanation Of The Diagram

(a) Hatchway, containing the companion way.
(b) Hatchway, with iron grille, guarded by a sentry.
(c) Another barred hatchway, also guarded by a sentry.
(d) Wall of boxes and packing cases.
(e) Passage-way and common room.
(f) Bench.

(g) Compartments divided into two, one above the other, each one being used as beds for eight convicts.

The two passage ways thus made on each side of the ship, being limited internally by the wall of boxes and packing cases, and externally by the side of the vessel, were about eleven and a half feet wide by a length, as already stated, of 75 feet. This width of eleven and a half feet was divided up as follows: 1 st, a clear space of three feet, the sole place where we could move about unrestrictedly, and even then it was only by walking with the head bent double, since the height between one deck and the other was not five feet; 2nd, a bench about eighteen inches wide which extended the whole length of the passage way; 3rd, a double row of compartments six feet deep which were to serve as beds for us.

These compartments, to the number of eighteen, that is to say, nine in each of two rows, one above the other, were seven feet and some inches square in front, with a depth, as already mentioned, of six feet. Each one was intended to receive four occupants. Some very coarse and extremely hard mattresses, if they can be called such, were placed on the bottom of these compartments or boxes, into which it was as difficult to crawl as it was to discover there a position that could be endured.

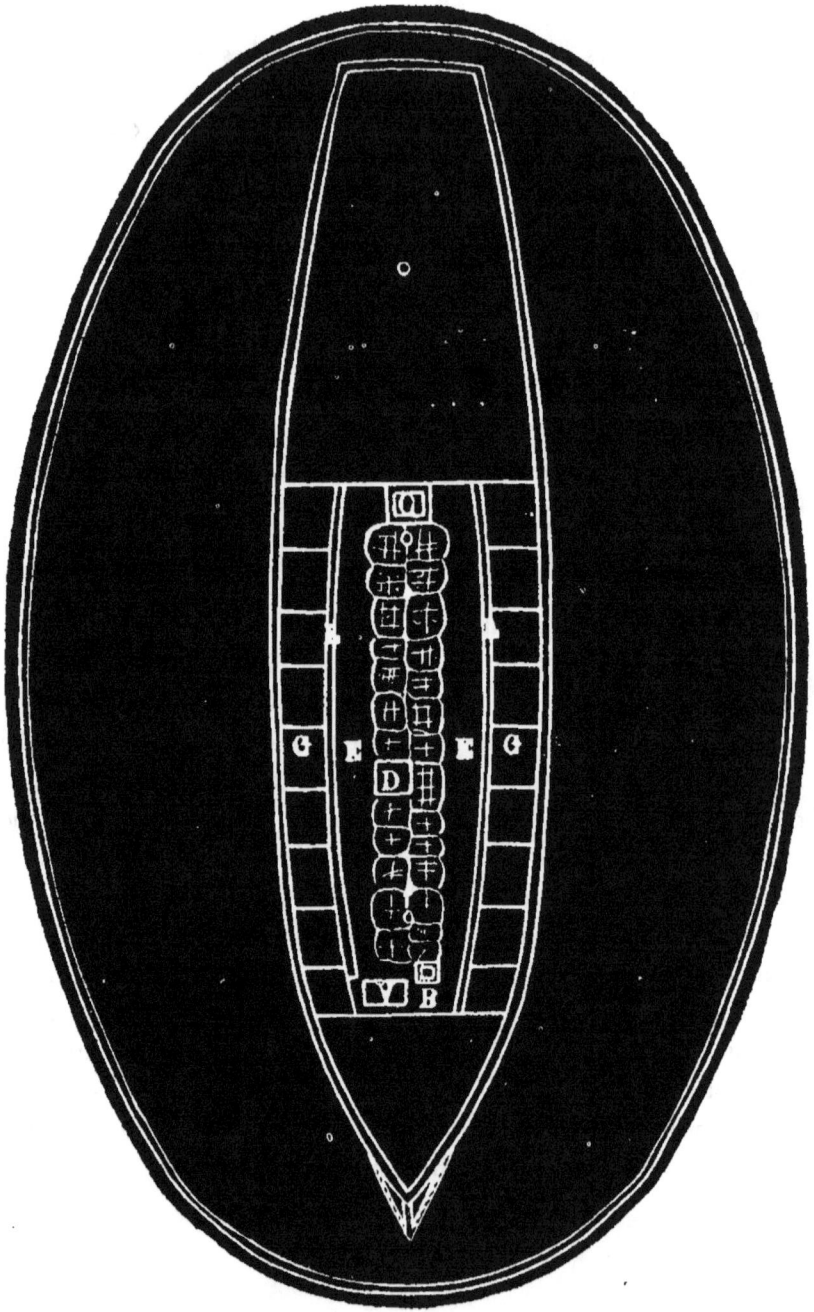

Plan of the *Buffalo*

We went below, into this frightful wretched hole, through a hatchway, about two feet square; then two sentries took up their positions at two other hatchways, strongly barred with iron grills, overlooking the two ends of our quarters, and communicating with the other decks of the ship, from above and down below. It was through these hatchways came the little light and air that we were permitted to enjoy.

The political prisoners from Upper Canada numbered 83; to these had been added three men condemned for murder, who were put in with us, bringing the total number to 144. The officers who had escorted us had divided us into two groups of 72 each; one was ordered to occupy the quarters on the starboard and the other those on the larboard side. My place on the bench I found was at the very end behind the starboard hatchway, where I had as my nearest neighbours Captain Morin, Mr. Morin, Jnr., Messrs. Huot and Lanctôt, the lawyers, Dr. Newcombe, and young Ducharme.

The bed which was allotted to me, that is which I was to share with three others, was that in the second row of the first compartment on the starboard side, and at the stern (alongside the hatchway marked "C" on the diagram.) It was in this compartment that the height between the two decks of which I have spoken was greater. From this place, it was necessary to step up in order to reach the general level of the deck which served as the floor of our prison.

Once installed, or rather stacked, with our little portmanteaux in this narrow, gloomy and stinking prison, we were served with a dinner composed of cold corned beef and biscuit; then we were left to our own sad thoughts, and to the terrifying forebodings that this kind of treatment naturally suggested.

In the evening supper was brought to us; it consisted of a clear oatmeal soup offered to us in a bucket, out of which with a cup we dipped about a pint, which constituted our regulation ration.

Immediately after supper we were ordered to go to bed at the sound of a bell which would ring every evening at eight o'clock; the hour for getting up was fixed for six o'clock. During the night absolute silence was to be observed. Communication, at any time, between one side of the quarters with the other was absolutely forbidden, and no one could visit the water-closets located on the upper between deck, near the companion way, without the sentry's permission.

At eight-o'clock we slid into the boxes which were to serve us as beds, four together, having only one blanket for two, and it already very dirty, and for a pillow a little cushion, very ill-made and terribly hard.

For my part, in spite of all the discomfort and distaste associated with a bed such as this, I slept well the whole night: it is true that I was worn out with fatigue and worry, and that, in addition, the cold that I had endured on the steamer had benumbed me to the point where I could in no wise feel the roughness of my sleeping quarters.

At the six o'clock bell the following morning, we came out of our boxes, somewhat bruised, slightly asphyxiated, and highly indignant at the way in which we were being treated. An officer went his rounds to check our presence in the passage way as he had done the evening before, to make sure of obedience to the regulation governing the hour of retirement.

Scarcely were we out of our beds than we heard the noise of the frigate's chains; the anchors were being raised, and very soon the vessel began to move. The noise of the steamer told us that we were being towed. We were setting out then on the great and painful voyage of exile; we were leaving our native land without being able to cast a last glance on that beautiful landscape of Canada, so lovely, especially in this magnificent seaport of Quebec, where we were at that moment. With common accord we went down on our knees and began to say together the morning prayer, a practice that we faithfully observed, morning and evening, throughout the whole length of the voyage. This first prayer was interrupted, for some few minutes, by the cannon shots fired by our ship, a salute to which the guns of the fortress of Cape Diamond replied.

About seven o'clock we were divided into groups of twelve to receive our rations. A bucket was the communal dish, intended to contain, turn about, or jointly, all our food; for the rest, we had neither knives, nor forks, nor spoons; the whole of our table equipment was made up of one small cup or pint measure.

The food ration was prescribed as follows: breakfast, a pint of oatmeal, slightly sweetened; dinner, four ounces of salt beef, four ounces of suet pudding and a few ounces of biscuit, or preferably (on alternate days) a pint of pea soup, three ounces of bacon and eleven ounces of biscuit; supper, a pint of cocoa, with whatever little biscuit remained over from dinner, whenever any did remain over.

The mess to which I belonged rejoiced in the luxury of a little pocket-knife which belonged to Captain Morin. This knife we used to cut up the meat that we scraped up with our thumb, after having drunk or eaten, according to our inclination, our pea soup out of the little panni kin. This is how, in the narrow 'tween decks that I have just described, during the long months of a voyage of several thousand miles, men who had never before known misfortune or necessity, men who, for the most part, had never seen the sea even in the distance, were compelled to manage.

As we could not be allowed to remain both day and night within the confined space of this floating prison, without the risk of seeing us all die within a very short space of time, a daily walk on deck for each of the prisoners was arranged as follows: each morning at nine o'clock one half of us, that is to say, seventy-two, were brought up on to the top deck and remained there in the open air until half past eleven (weather permitting) ; in the afternoon the other half occupied the same place on the forecastle at two o'clock and remained there until half past five.

During the first days of our voyage we had at least the final pleasure of seeing the North and South banks of the St. Lawrence. When, the first day, we went up on deck; we were a little below the island of Orleans, and the steamer which thus far had had our frigate in tow, had just cast off the tow lines. With envious eyes, for a long time, we watched it returning upstream, and approaching nearer and nearer to all those dear ones of ours from whom, we, the unhappy exiles, every minutes were moving farther away.

For five days the sea was calm and treated us kindly; but on the fifth day it became rough, from the effect of a strong wind; very soon sea sickness began to make its appearance amongst us. As the storm grew more severe, and the waves began to beat with greater violence against the sides of our ship, the number of victims of this horrible ailment increased.

The sixth day after our departure fifty-nine out of the seventy-two prisoners quartered on our side of the vessel were numbered amongst the sick, and we learned later that the state of affairs amongst the prisoners from Upper Canada, occupying the larboard passageway, was very much the same as ours, if not worse.

Those who have suffered sea sickness, or who have seen its effects, those persons alone can imagine in what condition we were, sick or not sick, deprived not only of light, but more especially of air, air so necessary for those who are attacked by the malady in question, crowded together in a narrow space and forbidden to make use of the beds, poor as they were, during the day time. The poor sick folk were compelled to cling desperately to anything available in order to reach the narrow bench from which the plunging of the ship, and their own weakness, continually flung them down upon the deck which had become wet, slippery and stinking through the vomitings.

Thirteen only, myself amongst the number, escaped the malady. For a whole week we had the painful experience of seeing our companions in the throes of this agony, which we endeavoured to alleviate as best we could. The rain, the wind and the rolling of the ship prevented, during the whole of this period, our taking advantage of the daily walk we had had during the first few days. The stench would have become overpowering, if it were not so already, had the precaution not been taken to place a tub in the 'tween decks which was situated above us, in the vicinity of the water closets. When the desire to vomit made itself felt, the strongest went to the tub, and of those who were not sick, six were constantly employed cleaning up our footpath, (This is the name that must be given to this deck), so as to dispose of the slops in this same tub. Scenes such as these were enough to upset one's heart, and 'I do not know how we were able to resist sufferings of all kinds such as these.

Add to all this the coarseness, the insults, even the brutalities of some members of the crew, amongst others those of a young officer of the name of Nibblett (I write this name as we used to pronounce it) who had scarcely any other names more courteous to apply to us than those of "son of a bitch," "cut throat," etc., etc. In view of this unworthy behaviour and of the treatment to which we were subjected, we came to the conclusion that the intention was either to bring about our deaths from distress and suffering during the voyage, or more probably to provoke us to some act resulting from despair which would give them an opportunity to decimate us. It must be confessed that ideas such as these were engendered by the manner in which we were treated in our period of great misfortune.

For a week then, our poor sick comrades had to undergo these terrible ordeals of sea sickness, and during the whole week we gave them freely all the care in our power, washing them, helping them to get up when they fell down, putting them into their beds in the evening and taking them out of them in the morning at the hour fixed by regulation.

At last, on the fourteenth day after our departure, it calmed down and fine weather reappeared. This particular day we were able to go up on the top deck so as to breathe the pure fresh air of the sea. Our poor sick ones now found themselves improved in health, and two days later there remained only five of our companions who still showed traces of the terrible complaint.

But another physical affliction awaited us at this stage of our journey. Sailors assert that "sea air gives an appetite." Oh! Well! Yes! Sea air and our week's semi-abstinence had the one result of considerably increasing our appetites. We had to be satisfied with the quantity of food .prescribed by regulation; consequently the majority of us had to suffer dreadfully during the whole voyage from malnutrition.

Persons other than ourselves, my comrades in exile and myself, will never be able to understand all that we suffered. At the present time, whenever I think of it, it is either like a dream wherein I love to feel myself freed from all my troubles, or like a nightmare which I am endeavouring to shake off, according to the state of mind in which I am.

It will appear to the reader that our situation was sufficiently distressing as to inspire in any human being no other emotion than pity, that our poverty and our misery were great enough as not to suggest the idea of adding anything more to it, that it should not come into the thoughts of anyone to improve his own position at the expense of unfortunates such as we were. Ah, well, nothing of the sort. There was amongst the personnel on board the ship a man who believed that he could take advantage, to his own benefit, of our unhappy state of impotence to carry out his own profits.

There was, on board the frigate, a person by the name of Black, a bankrupt merchant from Upper Canada, one who had obtained the privilege of a free passage to Australia on condition that he acted as our steward during the voyage; it was he who apportioned the prisoners' rations, and who had to supervise the cleanliness of our quarters. It came into the mind of this wretch to make himself look important to the authorities on board, and probably to obtain a reward, by cooking up against us the blackest and the most dastardly of all slanders. To accomplish his infamous scheme, he linked himself up with a prisoner from Upper Canada, a man named Tywell or Towell, who agreed, in return for promises of good treatment at the present time and of freedom at some future date, so serve as associate to this scoundrel.

Our worthless steward went then and sought out the commander of the frigate, during the morning of the fifteenth day of our voyage, to inform him that the Canadian and American prisoners (almost all the prisoners from Upper Canada were Americans) had formed a plot to mutiny against the crew and to take possession of the ship. Black pointed out Tywell, the prisoner, as one qualified to supply all the necessary information. The latter, summoned before the Captain, corroborated all that Black had said, as we found out later, and from this time the Commander of the ship, if he was not scared of a plot which would have been an act of complete madness on our part, had at least no further doubt about its existence.

We had not the faintest shadow of a suspicion of what was thus taking place with regard to ourselves; consequently no one can describe the astonishment that we felt when, at two o'clock in the afternoon of this same fifteenth day, we saw arrive at our quarters two officers, accompanied by strong detachments of the marines, who formed part of the crew, armed with pistols and cutlasses, just as though it was a matter of a boarding party. We received the order to proceed in silence towards the companionway which led to the 'tween decks, where we were placed under lock and key in a room about twenty-four feet square, situated in the bows of the ship.

We remained shut us in this place for about two hours, without knowing what they intended to do with us, and, unable to discover the object of this mysterious behaviour in reference to us.

When we came out of this second prison, whose approaches were guarded by men armed to the teeth, we received again the order to have no communication with one another on either side of our quarters, and to maintain, with more strictness than ever, the injunction to preserve silence. We were informed that the sentries had received orders to fire at the very first person who left his place without having previously obtained permission to do so.

During our two hour's internment in the storeroom of which I have just told you, all our bags had been opened, and all our beds turned upside down. Of course nothing compromising was discovered. Some pen-knives, razors and gold and silver coins, found in a few of the bags, were unmercifully confiscated. We found several of our cases smashed, our effects all topsy turvy and our miserable beds in a state of confusion.

In spite of the proof of the absence of any sort of plot, such was the result of these fruitless searches that the harshness of our treatment was redoubled, and that without allowing us the slightest opportunity of our justifying ourselves. We could not discover the cause of these raids and of this harshness. It was easy to see that we had been the victims of some false charges, but we could not imagine at first, upon what ground had been founded the suspicion of a "damned plot" of which, without any explanation except that which, with a flow of insults, the officer Nibblett directed at us. It was not until some days later that we learned the whole story, through the kindness of a poor sentry, moved by pity at the sight of the anxiety into which all this intrigue was throwing us. So as not to compromise this worthy fellow, we did not say a single word to the authorities of the disclosure that he had made to us, which, besides, did no harm to anyone; for the idea of a mutiny on our part was such an absurdity, as after reflexion could not fail to be obvious to everybody.

From this time, instead of sending us together everyday on to the upper deck, those on the starboard during two hours in the morning, and those on the larboard during two hours of the afternoon, we were compelled to go above only in squads of a dozen, and for one hour only; and even then we were compelled to stand in silence in a corner, under the supervision of an armed guard.

To add to our sufferings, very soon there came another evil, which very soon assumed frightful proportions; by which I mean lice, which; existing as germs in the beds arid bedding given us, had no difficulty in developing and multiplying in the conditions wholly favourable which our painful situation provided. We were soon covered with them.

The reader will pardon my giving these disgusting details, but I wish to give as complete a picture as a short narrative can provide of the sufferings that we endured.

The buckets from which our food was served were of an unbelievable filthiness; in our gloomy hell hole we could hardly make out what it was, except by the smell, but several times we could discover what it was by the look, when on the upper deck, when we were witnesses of the filthy methods employed to wash the buckets after the meal. May God forgive those who have treated us in this manner, even as I forgive them; but it is a sad thing for poor humanity to be compelled to point out acts of infamy such as these. Ah! readers from my own land, residents in our country districts and in our very Christian towns, you will never be able to imagine what we suffered, and my complete amazement, today, is that we were able to survive it. It is astonishing how much moral and physical suffering man can endure.

I have said a word about the insufficiency of our ration of food; but how many times did we see it reduced by accidents when conveying it from the kitchen to our dark, restricted quarters, especially during the days of violent winds, when the rolling and the pitching of the ship made walking so difficult on the ship's decks.

Once a week we set to work washing our clothes, during the hour which was given us, by turns, to spend upon the deck. This washing was done in salt water with a brush and a kind of pipe-clay, which took the place of soap, which could not be used with sea water. This job, important for us, had, in addition, the advantage of providing us with some distraction, and of tempering a little the boredom of our dreadful inactivity.

We had sick ones amongst us on whom we lavished all the care in our power; all of us, too, were terribly anxious, in our then state of fear, that we would not for long be able to stand up to our sufferings and to our privations of all kinds. We consoled ourselves with the thought of God, gaining fresh strength from prayer, the only solace of our misfortunes.

On the 15th October we had a general clean-up and washing out of our quarters, which were whitewashed with lime, a process which was repeated twice a week during the rest of the passage, for the dangers of disease increased the nearer we approached the warmer climates.

The false accusations of Black and the plundering of our possessions which followed in its trail had added still another misery to all the rest. If there is anyone amongst my readers who has ever undergone the torture of a shave made with a very bad razor, he will be able to gain some idea of the punishment which, twice a week, we had to undergo. On shaving days, we were brought up to the 'tween decks, where, each in his turn, we shaved one another with terrible razors, half eaten with rust, used by a large number of men, and in as bad a condition as possible. This procedure was carried out the whole course of the voyage, dating from the day on which the very few good razors of our own were taken out of our kitbags. The razors provided for communal use were entrusted to the care of our persecutor, Black, and at the end of the voyage it was almost impossible to endure the pain of the operation in question, which was always performed with cold water and without the help of a mirror, and often during the rolling of the ship brought about by a surging and tempestuous sea. I was, however, one of those who suffered least on this account, because of my youthful beard, then little noticeable and easy to cut; but certain of my comrades never returned from the operation in question without their faces bloody and their eyes streaming with tears.

As we approached the tropics the heat became stifling in our confined and airless quarters. For a whole month we were burnt up by the heat of the torrid zone.

Let one imagine one hundred and forty-four persons crowded together down in the depths of a ship's hold in a narrow space between two decks separated from one another by a space of only four feet and some inches, abandoned to perpetual darkness and only receiving air through two scuttles, supplied with canvas tubes to act as ventilators, subject to a food rationing detestable in every respect, having only one pint of water per day to quench an insatiable thirst, given over to myriads of insects, harmful as well as loathsome, and all that beneath a tropical sky and on the road to exile in the midst of criminals.

On our side of the ship we had about ten sick men, to whom no mitigation of treatment was accorded, and concerning whose fate we entertained grave doubts. We cared for them as best we could, but these attentions were only those of sympathy, for we had no material means of relieving them. On the side of the ship occupied by the prisoners from Upper Canada, there were even more sick. Even before reaching the tropics, on the 22nd October, one of them, the man named Priest, succumbed to his sufferings and was buried at sea.

These prisoners, whom we called the Upper Canada prisoners, were almost all Americans; among them were fewer than ten residents of Upper Canada. These men, who in 1837 and 1838 were distinguished by the name of "Sympathisers," appeared to me, so far as I was able to become acquainted with them through the relations we had, especially with those who formed part of our division, very respectable people. The state of emaciation and of destitution of these poor unfortunates was extreme; in spite of our own distress we recognised that they were still more unfortunate than ourselves, Then, too, we found in our faith resources and consolations which were lacking to the majority.

There were amongst us - I speak of the whole hundred and forty-four, some men weaker than others, amongst them one old man of more than sixty years of age with a chest complaint. To describe what these people, and especially this old man, had to suffer, would be an impossible task; a hundred times we thought that the poor old chap was upon the point of yeilding up his soul to his Creator. What a prospect for Catholics would it be to die without the help of a priest! But the God of all goodness hears our supplications, we say to one another, He is the witness of our desires, and He will accept our sacrifices by giving us prayers to make up for the absence of His minister if we have to perish in this vessel.

Amongst our sick people I shall make special mention of my friend, Mr. Hypolite Lanctôt, the lawyer, in practice today at Laprairie, on account of the close friendship which bound us together during our exile and which has never been broken since. Mr. Lanctôt, as I have mentioned previously, formed one of the same division as myself, and I was an eyewitness of his sufferings during the whole of the voyage; they were extreme. Time and again I believed him on the point of passing out. I made the most strenuous efforts, with the help of my comrades, to lavish on him all the cares of sympathetic kindness, in default of all those others which were lacking to us.

The walks that we made upon the upper deck (I mean by those who were able to go up there) were hardly any relief to us beneath the burning heat of the tropical sun. Entirely necessary as they were for the sake of our health, to tell the truth, they only seemed to make more noticeable to us the fever-laden air which predominated in our quarters.

Good-hearted people are to be found everywhere. We met some of them in the midst of the crew of the *Buffalo*. Two soldiers, much moved by so much wretchedness, had the humanity to bring to some sick men a little water with which they had mixed their ration of rum: caught one day in the act, they were both flogged. This severity, however, did not prevent another poor sailor on the rare occasions when he could do so, from bringing a little water to those who suffered most from thirst; but he used a high boot for his work of noble charity. Such was the need of drink which tormented us that this repulsive vessel did not prevent our finding this water delicious. These three men were not the only ones amongst the crew who showed compassion for us. They needed, in fact, to have accomplices in these acts of charity, for otherwise they would not have been able, even once, to accomplish their good deeds. Often we received marks of sympathy from some of the people on board the ship, but the orders and the control exercised by those in command were of a degree of cruelty which it would have been difficult to surpass. In spite of the severity of the authorities, we were still able, now and again, to procure a little water, provided, not this time by humanitarianism, but by the motive of filthy lucre. In return for the gift of some clothes from our very limited wardrobe, some sailors managed to bring us some water, collected in the ship's boats on deck during rainstorms.

9

A Stay in Port

After two months travelling we put into the Port of Rio de Janeiro, in Brazil. This break in our journey was necessitated by the need to procure provisions and fresh water, of which the victualling was not sufficient to see us through to the end of our voyage, not even to the ordinary ports of call, on account of the course taken, and the lack of speed made on our advance.

It was on the 30th November that we entered the fine roadstead of Rio-de-Janeiro. We enjoyed, during the few days of our stay in this port, a view of the magnificent scenery which there unfolded itself. During our walks (I have no other word for them) upon the main deck, we gazed at the peaceful waters of the vast bay, surrounded by lovely uplands crowned by lofty and picturesque mountains. With our eyes we followed the stylish little boats of all sorts which ploughed through the waters, and we felt inclined to envy the lot of the black slaves who handled these light skiffs.

These delightful scenes brought back to our minds the pleasant banks of the Saint Lawrence, and caused us to dream of the dear ones whom we had left, perhaps, alas! never to see them again, at any rate not in this world.

Our stay at the Port of Rio-de-Janeiro lasted for five days, which were of inestimable advantage to us; for, during this period, we were given a little more liberty, of which we took advantage to carry out some necessary cleaning operations; then the calm of the bay gave relief which had become necessary, especially for our poor invalids, from the tossing about and discomfort caused by the movement of the sea. But what gave us the greatest amount of comfort was that we had brought for us, but of the little money that had been confiscated, some fruit and other fresh supplies, which had, upon our debilated stomachs, the effect of a gentle balm upon a wound; it was time; for I sincerely believe that had it not been for this spell in port, several of my comrades, from both sides of the ship, would have died from distress and exhaustion.

In the port of Rio-de-Janeiro there were several vessels of the Royal British Navy; several officers of these ships came to see us. One of them, apparently of high rank, in our presence, asked our ship's officer who accompanied him, if we were subjected to the food ration prescribed for convicts, and received the reply, "Yes."

Did he ask this question so as to find a cause of complaint in case we should not have been subject to this regimen? Or did he ask it to indicate that we should not have been treated as criminals? I know nothing about it.

The *Buffalo*.

10

Across the Two Great Oceans

We set sail again on the 5th of December, and with the resumption of the voyage our sufferings were renewed. However, the wind was favourable, and it was not without a certain pleasure that we felt our ship cleaving the waves; for, although the fate that was awaiting us on the land of exile was an appalling one, nevertheless our primary concern at the moment was to be able to get away from this horrible ship, within whose sides all these tortures were inflicted upon us.

If, on the one hand, our condition was a little improved by the addition of a daily gill of lime juice to a slightly increased allowance of water, and by the diminution of the heat; on the other hand the lice multiplying in our clothing and in our beds caused us to suffer indescribable miseries. In addition to these symptoms of scurvy became apparent on some of us ; it was obviously this which caused the ship's officials to add a little lime juice to our rations.

The wind being continually favourable to us, by the 28th of December we had crossed the Atlantic Ocean and were off the Cape of Good Hope.

Two days later we were clear of these dangerous coasts, bordered with sandbanks and so frequently lashed by tempests, and had passed from the Atlantic into the Indian Ocean.

The year 1840 arrived ... How sad was New Year's Day for the exiles on board the ship *Buffalo*. What deep sighs we sent forth in the direction of our homeland, on this day that we knew would be so bright in our own dear Canada. Memories of childhood, family affections, all which passes through the memory am; the heart of man contended, in a spirit of sadness, for possession of our being ...

I give up trying to describe what was taking place within me; for, though I might pile up words and phrases, I could not succeed in expressing my thoughts. These things are felt, but cannot be described; at least I feel myself powerless to undertake a task such as this.

The treatment that we endured was always the same; it seemed that the young officer of whom I have already spoken allowed his harshness towards us to increase as he saw the time approaching when we were to be removed from his persecutions. To all the insults that hitherto he had showered up us he added the epithet, "stupid asses," which he often addressed to all those of us who could not understand or speak English, although he, himself, did not know a single word of French, the European language *par excellence*, the language of the courts and the salons, of science and diplomacy.

On the 8th February, 1840, we began to make out, on the horizon, the coastline of Van Diemen's Land; but then a contrary wind arose and, for four days, we had to tack about to reach the port of Hobart-town, within which we dropped anchors on the afternoon of 13th February.

The following day we learned that this colony was the place of destination of our travelling companions, the prisoners from Upper Canada: it was in this colony that they were to undergo the painful sentence which had been inflicted on them as on us.

Hobart Town, 1840 by George Augustus Robinson.

11

Hobart Town and a Noble Sol Pier

The little that I was able to see of the capital of Van Diemen's Land, from the deck of our ship, created a favourable impression of its situation. Houses and other buildings, in appearance, well-constructed of line; a magnificent harbour, which held at this time many ships, some of which carried flags foreign to England. A high mountain serves as a background to the scene and picturesquely dominates the town and the surrounding bushland.

On the 16th some boats manned by government officials came and hailed our ship; they came to get the prisoners from Upper Canada: the latter immediately received orders to take their places in these boats. By breaking the regulations a little, we were able to say goodbye to these, our unfortunate companions in misfortune. We were strangers to one another, strangers in religion, in blood, in language, and in customs; for the most part we were ignorant of their names; they were ignorant of ours; many of them could not make themselves understood; however, we shook their hands affectionately, our eyes, for lack of other means of communication, offered them our best wishes for their happiness. We felt that they were more unhappy even than ourselves.

During our stay in the harbour of Hobart-town we had a visit from a man whose name I am sorry I cannot give, but whose noble face will never be effaced from my memory. He was an officer of the English army stationed in this place; I do not know what was his rank, which, however, must have been a high one, to judge by the instructions about which he took the opportunity of speaking to us, and by the authority that his words seemed to carry with the ship's officers, who were apparently little pleased with his speech.

This worthy soldier, whose speech and manners revealed a perfect education, as a result of his interview with us, expressed signs of the most cordial sympathy. Passing through our ranks, saluting us with kindness, he told us to hope for better days. "You are not criminals," he said to us, "and your exile will not last forever." Then with a feeling of delicacy which thrilled us with gratitude, comparing our fate with that which had also befallen him, he told us that he, too, had been a prisoner of war when on active service in Spain: he had suffered the tedium and the miseries of captivity. Before leaving us, he concluded his kind action with these words which I reproduce from memory, but which I am quite certain are very close to the literal. "Gentlemen, you have no cause to be ashamed; I see nothing to tarnish your honour in the cause of your exile."

It is not possible to express all the happiness brought to the heart embittered by undeserved treatment by such gentle and noble words. It seemed to us that we were avenged for all the insults of Niblett and the harshness of other officers and personnel of the ship. Contrasted with the fine countenances, of our visitor, their miserable phizes invited pity. Henceforth we felt ourselves qualified to look down on them from a height; they were forced to lower their eyes. I should say to their credit that they really appeared to admit themselves humiliated.

We remained in the Hobart-town roadstead for five days, during which time we were provided with fresh meat and vegetables. This food did us much good, and such was the need of our poor debilitated stomachs that the quantities that were served appeared to us scarcely sufficient to appease our hunger. Our constitutions, ruined by our sufferings, and our poor bodies, gnawed by the vermin, had so much need of physical reparation that it was not just appetite that we were feeling, but, rather a ravenous, desire to eat.

12

Sydney and His Grace the Bishop of Sydney

On the 19th of February, about three o'clock in the afternoon, we left the port of Hobart-town, driven by a favourable wind, ploughing our way with all sails set: towards the place of our exile On the 24th we were In the latitude of Port Jackson, upon which is built the town of Sydney; but a strong adverse wind did not Permit us to enter the Parramatta River until the following afternoon.

We were in the depths of the ship's hold when the anchors were let go. The noise of the chains and the tramplings of the crew on the upper deck made our hearts rejoice; it was the announcement of an early release. It was not, however, the happiness that we expected to find upon this soil on which we were about to land; but it was the end, at least, of sufferings such as I believe if they could be any worse, it would not be possible for man to survive. We had endured during more than five months all the misery that the human heart and mind and body can endure at one and the same time.

We were then at the approaches to the town of Sydney, capital of New South Wales, where thrust into the midst of the major criminals of the United Kingdom was to be wasted an important part of our earthly existence.

Scarcely had an hour elapsed after our arrival than the worthy Bishop of Sydney, Monsignor Polding, accompanied by a missionary priest, Father Brady,[10] arrived amongst us. The benevolent prelate told us that, although quite unable to distinguish us, one from another, he knew everyone of us that we were his children, torn from the Church in Canada, but entrusted, henceforth, to the care of the church in New South Wales. The Bishops of Canada had written to Bishop Polding, and their letters of religion and charity had preceded us into these far distant regions of our harsh exile.

Monsignor Polding and his companion, Father Brady, who spoke French with the greatest of ease, remained with us for about an hour and a half, during which they lavished on us all the sympathy that the offerings of charity and priestly zeal could suggest. The Bishop informed us that he would come with some priests the following day, to receive our confessions; then, before leaving, he prayed for us and gave us his blessing. There is no necessity for me to attempt to express the comfort that this holy visit brought us, since these lines are especially intended to be read by my fellow countrymen, Canadians, children of the church, inheritors of the piety of glorious ancestors.

The following day Bishop Polding returned, as arranged, with two missionary priests. His Grace informed us that he had obtained from the authorities permission to celebrate mass in our wretched quarters, and that later, Holy Communion would be administered to those who were in a fit condition to receive it. We all made our confessions, preparing ourselves as best we could to receive our Saviour the following day.

As I have explained earlier, at one end of our narrow prison there was a space corresponding to a hatchway, within which the height between one deck and the other allowed several persons to stand erect. It was there that we set up, as well as lay within our power, the altar for the Holy Sacrifice.

On the 27th February, 1840, in the port of the capital of New South Wales, a Bishop of the Church of Jesus Christ, assisted by his missionary priests, celebrated the Holy Mass in the hold of a convict ship, and fifty-eight Canadian political exiles heard this mass, said for their benefit and received there the Holy Eucharist.

O, miracles of Religion! who can describe you! But if few possess the gift of revealing you, all have received that of feeling you, and it is especially to the unfortunate that this gift is accorded, in all its plenitude.

It was an unspeakable happiness for us to meet, on our arrival upon the soil of the land to which we had been transported, a protector, a father, in the person of a prince of the church, and friends so sincere in its worthy missionary priests. At that time we had great need of the help from on high that they brought to us, and of the power that is drawn from the Sacraments, so as to pardon wholeheartedly all those who, during this endless voyage, had shown themselves as cruel as they were unjust towards us.

The Holy Mass having been said, we all passed about half an hour in thanksgiving, after which the Bishop, placing himself in the midst of us, that is as far as the place would allow, and seating himself on our convict's bench, began to chat with us with solicitude and good-heartedness. First of all he congratulated us on the manner in which we had prepared the altar of which the ornaments' and the candlesticks had been provided by himself. The excellent prelate then discussed with us our actual fate, and of what might still be in store for us, giving us freely good advice based on religion and charity.

Bishop Polding told us that he did not believe that he should conceal from us that there was a rumour current to the effect that we were to be sent some hundreds of miles from Sydney, to a little island named Norfolk, christened in the colony with the name of "Hell on Earth." The prospect was undoubtedly a terrible one. This spot was at that time the place to which were sent the most depraved and incorrigible of the convicts. Every day the most atrocious crimes were committed there, and the treatment to which these wretches were subjected was in keeping with the character and the moral behaviour of the inhabitants of this frightful locality.

It seems that certain philanthropical institutions associated with the Canadian Government of the day had created an impression of us as exaggerated as it was vile: that, added to the effect produced by the lying and cruel articles in certain English newspapers published in Montreal, sent out to New South Wales, created the impression that we were personally linked up with bandits ready to attempt anything and to carry out the greatest outrages without a shudder.

The worthy priests who accompanied Bishop Polding vied with their worthy Bishop in their zeal to prepare us to accept, in the sight of God, the fate which awaited us, whatever it might be. The generous-hearted Prelate said a short prayer with us, repeated his episcopal blessing, and left us, saying that he was going, directly, to wait upon the Governor, to beg for us the favour of being landed in New South Wales.

The time of departure of these worthy ministers of religion seemed to us a veritable break; but already, inured to distress and misfortune, and strengthened by the bread of life, we prepared ourselves for the worst, practically certain that we were to be sent to Norfolk Island. We were resigned to everything, in spite of every difficulty in accommodating ourselves to the idea of taking our place amidst the vilest and most corrupt that the three kingdoms could supply.

Bishop John Bede Polding at the time he met the "Patriotes".

13

Inspection and Disembarkation

The ninth day after our arrival in Sydney Harbour, on the 5th March, we were advised that we were to be inspected by some government officials. This inspection began about three o'clock in the afternoon. We were assembled upon the forecastle, in parties of twelve, to present ourselves before three officials of the penal department. We were asked our name, our age, our birthplace, our religion, our profession, our standard of education. [11] They asked each one, in addition, whether he was married, whether he had any children, and if so, how many, whether he spoke English, etc., etc.

At the conclusion of these formalities, they sent us back into the hold of our ship, without addressing to any of us one word more than the plain cold questions written down upon the official documents; which, however, is less surprising when one keeps in mind that we were dealing with officials, whose duty it was continually to carry out the same work, and for whom we were merely convicts, and whose degree of guilt was augmented by all the exaggeration brought to it by the most blind and most deep-rooted racial and sectarian prejudices.

The following day, about ten o'clock in the morning, two other officials of the convict department came and subjected us to a second inspection. On this occasion a description of each of us was taken, each personal peculiarity being set down in detail, even to this extent that these gentlemen opened our mouths so as to examine our teeth, employing in this process almost the same formalities and the same amount of gentleness as a horse-dealer uses when ascertaining the age of a horse he thinks about buying.

Following on this second and very pleasant inspection, we were again led back into our hell-hole, where we racked our brains trying to guess what it was intended to do with us, as a result of all these proceedings and of this prolonged detention in our floating prison. All this confirmed us in the opinion that we were to be sent to the "Hell" of which the Bishop of Sydney had spoken.

This prolongation of our stay on board the frigate was a great disappointment for us, as well as a moral torture, resulting from the uncertainty concerning our destination. To the physical sufferings that we continued to endure were added the attacks of a kind of mosquito common in these parts of the world. These distasteful visitors had introduced themselves into our quarters and within a few days we were covered with little brownish lumps caused by their bites.

At last, on the 11th March, after a wait of two weeks in the port, we were informed that we were to go ashore, and that a boat was alongside the ship to take us there. Our preparations did not take very long; in a few minutes all was ready and ... we finally quitted the bowels of the pitiless *Buffalo!*

Our destination was a penal establishment situated eight miles from Sydney.

The protracted delays which had kept us so long on board the ship were due to the authorities' reluctance to admit us to the colony. To overcome this reluctance and to spare us the unhappy fate of exile at Norfolk Island, it had needed nothing less than the urgent and incessant applications of the excellent Bishop of Sydney. All these applications, however, would have remained valueless, in spite of a certificate of good conduct given by the captain of the *Buffalo,* if Bishop Polding had not pretty well guaranteed our future good conduct. It was a responsibility extremely difficult to be assumed by this excellent Bishop, who knew us only by the goodwill letters written in our favour by the Canadian prelates. But his charity triumphed over his uneasiness and he saved us from the horrible fate which was awaiting us.

Our destination was a place named Longbottom, on the Parramatta River. As soon as, with our baggage, we had taken our places in the boat which was to convey us, the sails were hoisted and we set out on our journey up the river, quite delighted to see close to us houses, trees and fields. It was about two o'clock in the afternoon when we came alongside the jetty at Longbottom. Then we were conducted, under a military escort, about a mile away from the river's bank. Our luggage, loaded on carts drawn by oxen accompanied us on the journey. We were so weak, so worn out, and so shaky on our legs that this short mile walk, taken at a slow pace, made us so tired that it gave us all pains in our limbs, pains that persisted with several of us for a few days.

A GOVERNMENT JAIL GANG.
Sydney N. S. Wales.

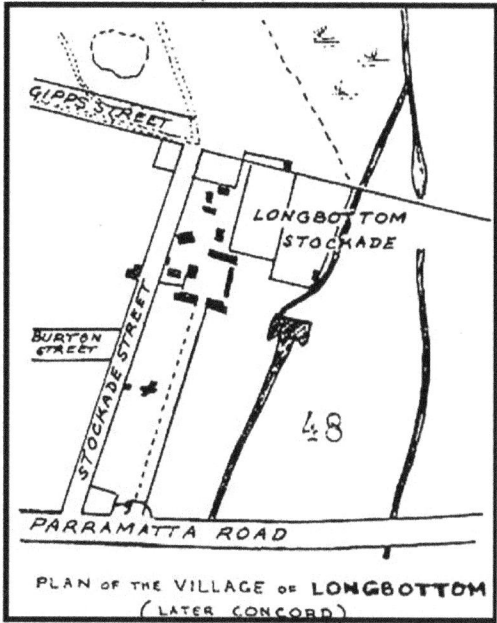

PLAN OF THE VILLAGE OF **LONGBOTTOM**
(LATER CONCORD)

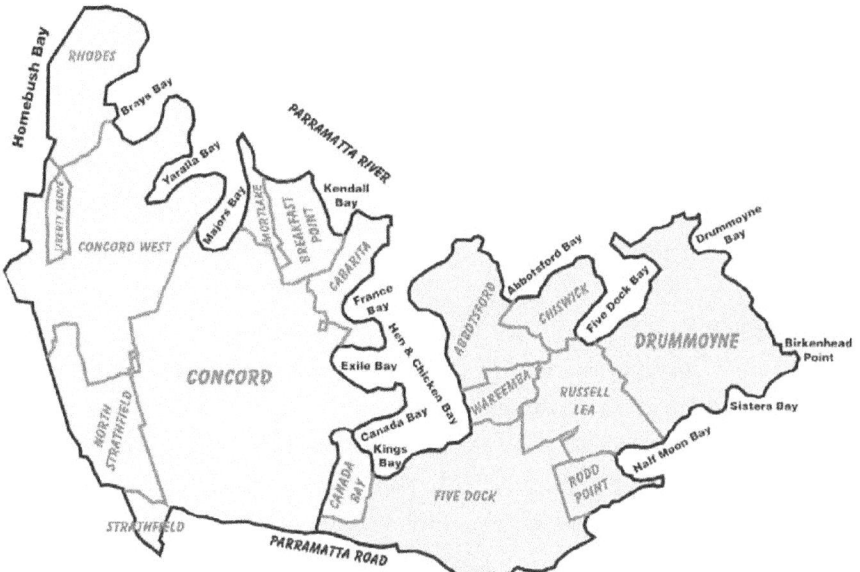

14

Longbottom and the Life Led There

The quarters which were allotted to us at our new home consisted of four shelter-sheds or huts, to which were added a little store-room, a kitchen, some other little buildings, and a barracks, at this time occupied by a squad of soldiers and some policemen. All these buildings were arranged in a square, the centre of which formed a courtyard which we were ordered not to cross without permission under the penalty of fifty lashes.

The behaviour and the language of our guards made us recognise pretty soon that they belonged to the same school as our persecutors on the *Buffalo*. In spite of that we felt ourselves truly happy to have left the gloomy sides of the tragic frigate.

To our group of fifty-eight were added four convicts, whom we found settled on the premises, and in such a way that we were lodged, fifteen or sixteen at a time, in each one of the four little prison-houses, which were about fifteen feet long by six feet wide. The four convicts whom I have just mentioned were placed with us as trustworthy prisoners. On them devolved all the minor duties; one of them even acted as messenger. It was easy to see that we were both objects of terror and of hatred in the eyes of the authorities, and that prejudices, false reports and ill-will had been completely successful against us. We made the strongest resolution to justify the confidence that Bishop Polding had placed in us, and to overcome, by our good conduct and our patience, all the unjust prejudices of which we were the object, so far at least as it was possible to obtain such a result from those with whom, unfortunately, we had to deal.

On arrival at our quarters, for our dinner we were served with a kind of meat pie, stingy enough in quantity, with which, however, we had to be satisfied.

A minute or two before sunset we were ordered into our narrow prison, while at the same time we were informed that there had not been time enough to prepare any beds for us, and that, consequently we would be compelled to sleep on the bare boards. It was then the season of the year which corresponds to winter in this country. At this period of the year the days still remain warm, when the weather is not stormy, but the' nights are cold and damp. It was one of these cold nights that, for the first time we had to spend, lying down, without any covering, upon the bare boards, with gaps between the joints, of our little huts. The result was that when, in the morning, about six o'clock, the locked doors of our quarters were opened, we were all discovered to have aching backs and heavy colds; some of us even felt seriously ill.

The daytime of the 12th, which was cold and wet, we passed inactively; but we were told that on the following day we would be taken to work.

Our food ration was detestable. Our breakfast consisted of a porridge made of maize flour, to which was added some brown sugar of an inferior quality. Our dinner of which the contents were to serve us also for supper, consisted of a half-pound of beef bought from Sydney in the worst possible condition, and about a dozen ounces of bread, badly made from the worst quality flour. As fresh running water or well water was lacking in the vicinity of our quarters, we were compelled to make use of rain water, collected in small reservoirs dug in the ground.

That evening, before we were again locked away in our huts, we were drawn up in a rank to be counted. We were again forced to sleep upon the bare boards without any coverings, a treatment which lasted until the first day of the month of May, During the whole of this time, on our own account, we used every effort to protect ourselves from the cold, by making use of all the effects left at our disposal and contained in our kit bags. We adopted every possible means of cleaning things up, and in this way, succeeded in ridding ourselves, more or less and gradually, of the vermin brought ashore from the *Buffalo*.

On the 13th, after having passed through the same experiences as on the evening before, advantage was taken of a second day's rain, which prevented outside work, to subject us to a procedure which put the finishing touch to the process of classing us with the convicts. We were made to stand in a line, and two officers of the establishment, one carrying a pot of black paint, the other a branding iron, moved up and down our ranks, stamping our clothes on the back, the legs, the arms and the chest with the letters for penal servitude. These letters, "L.B.," were the initials of the name of the establishment that we were occupying, Long-Bottom. [12]

At the conclusion of this business we returned to our little huts, there to swallow, in the privacy of our own quarters, the shame with which we were overwhelmed. Amongst us were three veterans of 1812, one of them who had fought at Chateauguay, and who had not received the rewards and distinctions promised, and which have only been granted since to the survivors of this period, displayed extraordinary indignation at seeing himself thus decked out in convict's livery. "Be content," said one of us to him, with the bitterness inspired by indignation, "it is the decoration that was promised you, your cross of honour."

In the afternoon, the weather having improved, the Superintendent of the establishment, whose name was Baddly,[13] ordered us to make ready to go to the stone-yard. This we did at once, under the direction of the warders, and the superintendence of a squad of armed soldiers. Furnished with picks, shovels, hammers and wheel barrows, we set out for the scene of our operations. Our working place was located about twenty-five acres away from our quarters, on the bank of a little bay of the Parramatta River. Our task consisted in preparing the macadam for the neighbouring main roads. Some of us were set to work digging the stone out of the quarry; some to transporting it in wheel-barrows, and others still to smashing it up on the heap formed for this purpose. As one of the youngest and most vigorous, I was set to the barrows, and I assure readers that I carried out my task conscientiously. I even derived pleasure from the hard work, and in performing the duties attached to my unhappy condition. I do not believe that the authorities have any complaints to make against us on this score. We well and honestly earned the poor bread and meat which were given to us.

About six o'clock we received the order to gather up the tools, and to form ranks again to march back to the camp, where we should find no supper - for at mid-day we had eaten the whole of the pittance given to us for the whole day, less a few scraps of meat that we could not touch - nor a bed to lie upon.

In accordance with the order recently received, nothing in the form of bed-clothes, clothing or boots could be given to us until the first of May. We were sufficiently supplied with clothes, but our shoes were very soon unserviceable. The five and a half months wear and tear during our passage across the Atlantic and the Pacific had already had some effect on them, but the use to which they were subjected on the stones and rock work of the quarry at Long Bottom was almost the whole cause of it.

For myself, having to walk continually over the crushed stones, I very soon saw myself almost bare-footed, which, it is easy to imagine caused me much suffering, especially during the first few days. Often the blood oozed from the wounds and the blisters with which my poor feet were covered.

The monotony of the tasks of a prisoner do not lend themselves readily to recital, consequently the description that I have just given of our work and of our miseries during one day will adequately resemble that of each day which passed from our arrival at the establishment of Long-Bottom, until the day when we were allowed to leave it, except for the variety created by the somewhat rare events that I am now about to describe.

On the first of May took place the distribution to us of the clothing provided by the State. These garments consisted of a coarse cotton shirt, a pair of trousers, a jacket and a grey cloth cap, heavy shoes with strong soles provided with broad-headed nails (no stockings were provided). All these things bore that mark of the Ordinance Department that is called crow's foot, and in various places the initial letters of the name of the establishment "L.B."

In this region, for us, the whole world was turned round about; summer time had become winter time, southerly winds, bringing cold replaced our northerlies, because, though these latitudes have no snow, they are not without cold; the natural productions were quite different from those to which we were accustomed in our own beloved Canada; the manner and habits of the people, as much as we could judge of them through our rare contacts with the outside world, all appeared strange to us, and all made us sigh for and wish for our native land.

One thing alone preserved the same character as in our own dear country of Canada, religion! We found in the excellent missionary priest who visited us from time to time, Father Brady (since elevated to a Bishop in Australia) the same doctrine, the same sentiments, the same charity, even the same language as in our Canadian clergy. So what a treat it was for us when this good priest came amongst us.

Bishop Polding himself came twice to see us during our sojourn at Long-Bottom, and on each occasion he celebrated Holy Mass at our settlement. The Saviour of men came into the world in a stable, and it was still in a stable that He came to visit the Canadian exiles of Long-Bottom. This parallel, which struck me then, rendered these pleasant hours more delightful still! Let me explain.

There was, amongst the buildings which surrounded our dwellings, a little shed of which I forgot to speak previously, but which served both as stable for the horses, and as dining room for us, It was the only one of our buildings that we could convert into a chapel, and it was in this stable, cleared and decorated by us, that twice, during our stay at Long-Bottom, the Lord and Saviour descended in, the voice of his Vicar on earth, the Bishop of Sydney.

For each of these two occasions we taxed our ingenuity to decorate this humble little lodging, after having cleaned it, as best we could, fine large fern leaves, gathered in the bush, decorated with this greenery the whole interior of our chapel; the wall face at one end of the building, where the altar was raised, was covered with a cotton cloth adorned with all the little holy pictures, presents from our families, brought with us from Canada in our baggage. A table built from pieces of wood covered over with a cotton cloth formed the altar upon which were placed a crucifix and two candle sticks holding wax tapers, brought from Sydney by Bishop Polding … It was in this improvised temple that we had the consolation of participating in the holy sacrifice of the Mass, and of receiving, as nourishment, the angel's bread, from the hand of his Grace the Bishop of Sydney.

During these kindly visits of Bishop Polding and of the Rev. Father Brady, these worthy clergymen did not fail to pass as much time as possible with us, so as to console us, and to exhort us to accept with patience, in the sight of God, all our miseries, They interested themselves also in our temporal welfare, and tried every means in their power to procure some comforts for us; but the Governor, Sir George Gipps, for some reason or other, so it appears, did not feel any sympathy for us. Because he had granted Bishop Polding the favour of admitting us to New South Wales instead of banishing us to Norfolk Island, he doubtless, believed himself exempt from all feelings of charity as far as we were concerned.

During one of his visits to our establishment, Father Brady conceived the idea of sampling our dinner, which he found very bad and insufficient. Impelled by the desire to be of some use to us, by awakening in our favour humanitarian feelings which might possibly exist in the hearts of the population of the country, the good missionary priest sent to a Sydney newspaper the name at which has unfortunately disappeared from my notes, and which I have forgotten, a letter of which the following is the translation:

THE CANADIAN PRISONERS

The Editor,

I have just this minute returned from Long-Bottom, where I spent two days with the political prisoners from Canada. His Grace the Bishop has also visited them, he has given them his blessing, and has encouraged them to endure patiently their exile, and all the misfortunes which are inseparable from it.

When I consider the courage of these prisoners, and their spirit of resignation, I cannot conceive how men so gentle, so modest and so good, whose conduct arouses the admiration of all those who are witnesses of it, can have deserved so terrible a punishment.

They have had the misfortune to see themselves snatched from the arms of their wives and children; they have seen their homes and their possessions given over to pillage and to destruction by fire, and after months of anguish, fear and shattered hopes, spent in the depths of prison cells, they received the terrible sentence which to separate them from all they held dear in the world, so as to cast them into banishment in a far distant soil, where they are suffering through being deprived of the most necessary things. The food that they receive is so bad that the white Irish slave,[14] accustomed to living on potatoes and salt could scarcely put up with it; in spite of this, the settlement at Long-Bottom costs the Government nearly a thousand pounds sterling per annum, an expense that could be saved by granting these men permission to seek employment in the colony, or, at the least, by assigning them to good masters.

If you think that these remarks have any importance, will you be good enough to insert them in your useful and excellent newspaper; by so doing you will oblige

Your obedient servant, J. BRADY,

Missionary-Priest.

The editor of the paper to which this communication was sent accompanied its insertion by some very sympathetic remarks, very similar to those in the letter itself of the excellent missionary-priest. But the author of the letter was an Irish priest, the newspaper was a Catholic journal, and the victims French Canadians, with the result that the total effect was to direct on us, on the part of another Sydney newspaper (*The Sydney Herald*) a flood of insults and slanders. According to this *veracious, charitable* and *honourable* writer of the *Herald*, our whole career in Canada had been marked out by murder, pillage and arson. We were, each and everyone of us, only cut-throats worthy of a fate a hundred times worse than the inflicted on us; to sympathise with us was to sympathise with crime ... in a word, all that such a newspaper could invent relative to such a matter.

We were still compelled to suffer all this, without uttering a word, and to endure the thousand little 'irritations that such articles, swallowed by a public ready to receive them, did not fail to bring upon us.

The choice of the officers and warders of the transportation department, in the penal colonies of England, is not always of the best, if one can judge them by my experiences as a political convict in New South Wales. The superintendent of the establishment at Long-Bottom was a coarse, brutal man, whose manners were detestable and whose temper almost as uncontrollable as uncontrolled. We learned from his subordinates, who hated him at least as much as they feared him, that he had been an officer in the army from which he had been dismissed on account of misconduct.

This man took pleasure in setting traps for our patience, and he had especially got his knife into Mr. Huot, on account, I suppose, of his advanced years, his professional character, and of his particularly distinguished appearance. Our Superintendent never failed to take advantage of the opportunity of trying to provoke us, and thus to induce us to be lacking in respect towards him; but we were on our guard, and with the keenest desire in the world to catch us in the wrong, he did not often so succeed. I might even say never, in the strictest and most exact meaning of the word.

George Street, Looking South, Sydney 1842, by Henry Curzon Allport.

15

An Adventure and It's Consequences

However, one peculiar circumstance changed the behaviour of our Superintendent towards us. Dating from this time, his ill-will gave place to confidence. This is how the affair took place, and it is worth the trouble of being narrated.

As I have already said, our guard was made up of one squad of policemen, and one squad of soldiers. Several of these men were married, and our Superintendent was a bachelor, having so little respect for himself that he was pretty indecent. One evening when the Superintendent and his cronies had gathered together in one of the rooms where his policemen resided with their families, to drink and enjoy themselves, it happened that the worthy chief and his worthy subordinates became so blind drunk that the differences of ranks and grades could no longer be distinguished. The Superintendent, having so far forgotten himself as to publicly insult the wife of one of the policemen, the husband of this latter attacked his captain hammer and tongs, and showered on him a succession of punches which then restored to the latter his sense of authority. Then he ordered his subordinate officers to arrest the assailant and to take him off to the clink, a dark cell made for prisoners undergoing solitary confinement.

It must be understood that some took the side of their chief, and that others sided with the insulted husband, for a terrible row then took place. From our dormitories we heard the yells and the noise of the smashing of furniture and crockery in the midst of the brawl.

In the embarrassing position in which he found himself, our Superintendent, forgetting his prejudices and his unjust restriction, rushed towards our little cells, opened the doors and summoned us outside. This we were able to do without any delay, owing to the fact that, by reason of the cold and the lack of bed-clothes, we were lying down, as usual, fully-dressed. Once assembled, which was the work of only a minute, the Superintendent ordered us to arrest all the policemen and all the soldiers, and to lock up, in one of the sheds, the whole force appointed to guard us. We obeyed, without knowing then a single word about the origin and causes of the quarrel, and without foreseeing what would be the consequences of this extraordinary adventure. Only one man, a sergeant, had been exempted from arrest. It was he alone who was charged with the duty of guarding us during the rest of the night.

That i s h ow w e gained t he good g races o f o ur superior, t o such an extent that we ventured to represent to him that our bed-clothes Were insufficient during the cold nights, and that on our behalf he caused representation to be made to the government, and showed himself very displeased with the refusal which followed his request.

On their arrival in this country, very few foreigners escape dysentery, it goes without saying that we, under the conditions that I have described, did not escape it. Several of us even were very ill as a result.

In the midst of all these afflictions, ou r pa tience, ou r su bmissiveness, triumphed at last, up to a certain point, over prejudices, malevolence, and calumny, At the end of three months the authorities withdrew the armed force which guarded us so effectively, a nd we were left alone at Long-Bottom, under the control of our Superintendent, who had fewer complaints against us than against his own men, and who, from the very beginning, knew well that we were not criminals.

The duties of overseers, night-warders, door-keepers, cooks and servants were given to those of us who were least accustomed to manual work, or to those who seemed to the Superintendent the most suitable to carry them out. As for myself, I was made night sentry with Mr. Huot, the lawyer.

It can be understood that this radical change improved our situation considerably. There was nothing, right down to the cooking which did not feel the effects of it; our food was selected with greater care and cleanliness, and infinitely better prepared that previously; but it was especially exerted in friendly feeling, so that this change exercised over us a tremendous degree of relief. Moreover, it will easily be imagined that, without failing in our duty to our tasks we were able to permit ourselves a host of minor liberties which previously were forbidden us, under most severe penalties. Our Superintendent, who had become less coarse and less brutal, used to go to sleep whenever he felt inclined, so great was the confidence that, by our good behaviour, we had been able to inspire in him. I have already told how greatly at night in our little cells, we used to suffer most frequently from the cold, sometimes from the heat, and always from the polluted air; taking advantage of the freedom which the new state of affairs permitted us to enjoy, we were able to bring some relief to this distress. By opening the doors of our quarters, we were able to warm ourselves at a fire built in the kitchen during the cold winter nights, and to take the air during the warm summer evenings. Our cook had found out the way to make, out of scorched maize flour and the meat of our rations, stews infinitely preferable to the disgusting gruel and to the unsavoury boiled beef of our former ration.

Shortly after the withdrawal of the guards, our Superintendent permitted us, between the regular set hours of hard labour, to undertake a little private work, which consisted of collecting, on the shore of the bay[15] near which we were working, some shells which we sold to the lime-burners, for in this country lime is manufactured from shells which are to be found in abundance on all the beaches. In this way we were able to obtain a few pence with which we bought a little rice and sugar for our Sunday dinner.

As the ration of Indian corn supplied by the Government for the working bullocks was more than sufficient, we were able to make profitable use of the surplus, which our warders previously used to sell for their own benefit, by converting it, by a process of grinding and roasting, into a kind of coffee, from which we prepared a beverage, which our readers will imagine, and with good reason, to be abominable, but which, nevertheless, was of much greater value than the unchanged water in our tanks.

With the warm summer season came the Australian mosquitoes, the worst of all the mosquitoes in the world, according to the unanimous opinion of all travellers who have visited New South Wales. We had to suffer terribly from them; the site of our establishment, the construction of our quarters, and the total absence of the means usually taken to diminish the effect of this plague, made us early victims of the viciousness of these cruel insects. The plague of which I speak is such that the use of gauze mosquito nets for beds is general in this country; in fact this article is counted amongst the essentials. Needless to say that we hadn't any.

After being employed for about six months breaking stone, as I have mentioned earlier, we were then sent, some of us, to drag this same stone on to the road from Sydney to Parramatta, others to *cut* wood blocks for paving the streets of the town of Sydney. All these works were carried out without the interference of anyone at all, with the exception of our Superintendent, who merely gave us general orders, leaving to us the duty of carrying them into effect. It was, as can be seen, an entirely different set-up, which effected a complete change of opinion on the part of those who were invested with authority: this change, however, did not take place without exacting protests, more or less malevolent, from people who persisted in wishing to confuse us with the great criminals with whom these penal colonies are filled, and where they very often commit horrible depredations. However, as the government derived some credit from the new order of things, and as nothing inconvenient had resulted from the confidence that had finally been reposed in us, we were this time freed from the foolish statements uttered in the newspapers and repeated by the credulity, evil-minded as well as ignorant, of a certain section of the public.

Convicts being marched to Longbottom stockade.

16

A Chapter that begins and Ends with death

In the course of the second year of our sojourn at LongBottom, two of our comrades became so ill that it was necessary to transfer them to a hospital situated eight miles away. Gabriel Ignace Chèvrefils was attacked by an inflammation of the bowels, and Louis Dumouchel by dropsy.

Chèvrefil's complaint, according to the opinion of our companion, Dr. Newcombe, who, in addition to his forced labours, practised his art amongst us with all the benevolence possible, was due to starvation, following on a change in diet. This splendid honest and religiously-minded companion, was of colossal stature, and endowed with an extraordinary appetite in proportion to his size, an appetite which he had never been able to satisfy since our departure from Canada, although occasionally he received a small portion of food, sometimes from one, sometimes from another of his comrades, who, however, had hardly enough of it for themselves. One evening, having procured a certain quantity of this roasted Indian corn of which we made a kind of coffee, overcome by the pangs of hunger, he ate it, and it was this which caused the illness I have just mentioned.

Chèvrefils and Dumouchel were moved to the hospital after an interval of several weeks. As long as it was possible, Dr. Newcombe had lavished all his care on these two unfortunate comrades; but his medicine chest containing only a few purgatives and our food ration permitting no change of diet, we were compelled to accept separation from our poor friends. As I have stated, the hospital was eight miles from our establishment, that is to say, within the boundaries of Sydney; it was a hospital set apart for convicts.

Our two unfortunate comrades were carried off, lying on straw, in a cart drawn by a bullock. We settled them as comfortably as possible in this rough vehicle, and we each shook their hands with tears in our eyes, for we felt that this was the last farewell. They did not recover from their illnesses; both died up on a foreign soil, Chèvrefils, I believe, only five days after his removal, and Dumouchel about a fortnight. Our only consolation was the belief which we then held, that they were escaping at one and the same time from the two states of exile that they were suffering together, and were about to enjoy the delights of heaven, of which no one could deprive them. We were afraid, a little while later, that once again we should have to be separated from another comrade who was suddenly seized by excruciating pains in his bowels, after having eaten a piece of tainted meat from our rations, but he recovered after some days of suffering, during which time he remained stretched out helpless on his straw bed.

We had been twenty months at Long-Bottom when the order arrived permitting us to hire ourselves out to the residents of the country, according to the custom in force in the Australian penal colonies. The convicts, to whom we were in every respect similar, when they arrive in these penal colonies, are at first employed on public works on behalf of the Government, as it has just been mentioned, we were. In the usual course of events, it is only after a couple of years of this type of work that these unfortunates pass to another phase of their life as transportees ; then they are *assigne* (assigned) - that is the translation of the English word which is used - to residents of the country who benefit by their work, receiving in return their food and a small wage. From this moment, the convict ceases to be a burden on the Government, but he remains under the supervision of the police, having as the limits of his gaol his master's property, or the range set out in his contract of hire. Later on, the convict who has not committed any infraction of the law, is allowed to work for himself; then finally he obtains his freedom and becomes a citizen of these Australian colonies. In this way it very often happens that a convict finds himself assigned to a former convict who has become a landowner, sometimes very wealthy, sometimes occupying more or less important public positions, and occasionally one of the most respectable citizens in the land.

The conditions governing our assignation were: 1st, that we should be employed at work commensurate with our strength, our skill and our previous occupations; 2nd, that each one of us should be paid seven shillings and six-pence per week, of which three shillings and ninepence were to be given us for our maintenance, and three shillings and nine-pence, as a nest-egg for our future, to be deposited in a Savings Bank; 3rd, that we were to receive ten pounds of fresh beef, ten pounds of wheaten flour, one pound of sugar and four ounces of black tea each week as our rations.

The assigned convicts are themselves obliged to prepare and cook their food, and they are quartered in little huts separated from their master's residence, somewhat in the manner of the negro slaves in the American plantations. The meal hours were as follows: breakfast at seven o'clock in the morning, dinner at noon, and supper at the end of the day's work, which lasted from six to six, with an hour for cooking and eating breakfast and an hour for dinner.

The assigned convict is forbidden to leave his master's property after his working hours. For going out on Sunday he must carry on his person a written permit bearing his master's signature; without this precaution he is almost certain to be arrested by the mounted police who ceaselessly patrol the country to protect the inhabitants against the attacks of the bushrangers, or convicts who have broken bounds who often unite into bands and wander over the country, giving themselves over to all sorts of excesses and crimes.

It is not only the assigned convicts who are thus compelled to give proof of their regular behaviour, but the half-freed convicts, that is, the ticket-of-leave men, and the free men themselves are forced to carry safe-conduct passes if they do not wish to risk arrest; for when a crime has been committed, the mounted police do not stand upon very much ceremony (at least such was the case at the time of which I speak) ; they arrest all those who are not known as citizens, or who are not in possession of passes or safe-conduct certificates. The moral condition of these people renders these measures absolutely necessary. Very often it is only the convict dress which distinguishes the colonist from the criminal; besides the former criminals who are now free men, there is a crowd of people who, in order to escape legal conviction by exiling themselves to the southern lands, have executed justice on themselves. However, there are to be found, in this colony so unpleasant socially, some citizens of the highest worth, so that one cannot understand why they have selected these colonies as their adopted country. There are even former convicts who are, at heart, very fine folk, for those whom human justice mixes together under the name of convicts are not all of the same rang before God, nor of conscience and honour, taking into consideration also that many have been the victims of error, others the victims of injustice.

However that may be, the Canadian political convicts had been notified that they were about to enter on a new phase of their Australian career; they were about to become things to be hired out, true slaves. Nevertheless it was a great improvement in our condition, and the only thing which troubled us at this piece of news was the thought that we were about to be separated from one another.

Gradually we had all passed from the settlement at Long-Bottom to the properties of our new masters. One alone of us was still at Long-Bottom, when by a peculiar coincidence, our Superintendent, whose health for some time had been on the decline, became seriously ill.

Providence had decreed that he should not survive the departure of his former prisoners. He died in the charitable arms of the last Canadian left with him. No other person came to be present with him in his last moments, and not a single friend followed his coffin to the cemetery. His funeral was no different from that which, in these penal colonies, is accorded to the mortal remains of a convict. The bier was carried on the same hard, rough cart, drawn by the same bullock which had conveyed our two poor comrades to the hospital. The cortege comprised only the Canadian who drove the vehicle, and a Protestant minister who, not uttering the prayers for the dead, had come there to read some useless verses from the Bible, to which no one responded.

17

How I Became a Confectioner

As for myself, I was at first hired out to a Frenchman, a native of the island of Mauritius. He had not hired me alone; there were two of us, my companion in slavery being Mr. Louis Bourdon. Our new master was not one of the cream of the population of the island of Mauritius; it was easy to perceive that from his language and his manners. He had hired us with the ostensible aim of employing us in his factory, but in reality with the idea of speculating in connection with our employment, for, scarcely had a few days passed than he hired us out again at a profit to two of his associates, a Frenchman and a German, who had recently arrived in Sydney with the intention of opening there a confectioner's shop.

The shop was not yet ready. For three weeks we worked with our masters in a shed, where we slept, manufacturing syrups, sugar candy and other articles which were intended to adorn the shelves of the proposed sweetshop and tickle the palates of the Sydney-siders.

Such an occupation was something new for us; I hope that our masters' customers found our syrups delicious; in any case we did our best, and we hold ourselves responsible only for our part of the job, which we carried out conscientiously.

During the temporary state of our masters' establishment, we were very badly accommodated, in the company of an army of rats of extraordinary effrontery; but we were well and abundantly fed. You should have seen what justice we did to the good table kept by our masters. We were almost ashamed to display so much satisfaction in eating. But it was really the cries of delight from our poor stomachs. In a word, our new situation, although little enviable in itself, since we were, after all, only slaves, wearing the convict uniform, our new situation was an earthly paradise compared with the years through which we had just passed.

At last, after three months factory work, our masters and ourselves set to work to stock up the shop by displaying, upon the shelves of a small shop that had been rented, the syrups, the cakes and the sweets.

It happened then, that my companion, Mr. Bourdon, and I were separated from one another, or almost so, on account of the different type of work which was allotted to us. Mr. Bourdon, knowing English better than I, was placed behind the counter, where, under the direction of the French partner, he met the whole fashionable world of Sydney, whereas I remained with the cooking pots, in company with the German, who, as he was the more skilled of the two partners, was not the more pleasant tempered one.

I had little aptitude for cooking, still less for confectionery, consequently whipping eggs, stirring creams, crushing sugar and scouring saucepans were for me very little attractive occupations, but there it was, I was a slave and I had to obey. I can even do myself this justice and say that I always did my best in the interest of my masters and of the public they served.

However, in spite of all the pains taken by our masters, and in spite of our efforts to give them good service, affairs did not go as well as was expected, and our German, especially, did not become more pleasant. After the first month that I spent with these masters, I had been allowed to go, without any interference, to Mass with Mr. Bourdon: the first Sunday following our separation, caused by the difference in our work, things were not the same. As I was preparing to set out with my companion, the German came and told me that he needed me to work in the shop, saying to me, in his, abominable French, that he recognised neither holidays, nor Sundays, that he worked every day that the sun shone and that he was determined that I should do the same. I replied that I was ready to obey him in everything that was lawful, and permitted by my conscience, but that I would not work on Sundays. I added that, by the regulations, Sunday was reserved for rest, and that, in the presence of the men themselves he had no right to force me to work on this particular day, during which my duties towards God called me elsewhere than to his factory. As he insisted, I told him I would go, that very day, to my first master, from whom he had hired me, so that he might cancel the bargain entered into with him, and that, if need were, I would approach the proper authorities concerning my difficult situation.

After Mass I actually did seek out my master, the Frenchman from the island of Mauritius, and told him my story. The latter agreed concerning my right to refuse to work on Sunday, but he added that he had nothing to give me to do, and that, if I could not make suitable arrangements with the confectioners, he would be compelled to send me back to the Government. I then made up my mind to go myself, the following day, to the office of the Government department concerned, in order to forestall the report that my first master must lodge there, and to plead my cause as best I could.

I did not sleep very peacefully that particular night so greatly did I fear having any dealings with the Government officials. It was, therefore, not without qualms that on Monday morning I crossed the threshold of the office mentioned, immediately after the door was opened. I asked to see the head of the department, in person, and I was ushered into his presence. I confess that I had little confidence in this proceeding, even the results of which I feared. But it was a question of which I wished a solution there and then.

The head of the department was a former army officer, whose name was Captain McLean. I told him that I was one of the Canadian exiles, and I was about to relate to him my whole story, in my very poor English, when he said, with politeness and marked signs of sympathy, speaking to me in very good French, that I could use my mother tongue to explain to him my business.

With this great gentleman I had a long conversation, which, for me, was a truly moral tonic, if I may so express myself. For some years my feelings and my human dignity had been so frequently hurt that I did not feel myself at ease when facing a man of superior education, whose heart and intellect were on the same level as his position. This interview reconciled me a little to my environment, and filled me with hope for the future. I am happy to present for the blessings of those who will read these lines the name of Captain McLean.

I told my excellent interviewer about the transaction by which our first master, the Frenchman from Mauritius, had hired us out to the confectioners, how we had served these latter zealously, faithfully and obediently, right up to the moment when the German had wished to compel me to work on Sunday.

After having listened to me courteously, Captain McLean gave me to understand that in accordance with the usual practice, a hired convict, sent back by his master to the Government because of disputes, was returned to a penal establishment to work there for the Government until such time as a new master could be found for him, but, he added, that he would not take any such action regarding me; that he knew well how to differentiate between the Canadian political exiles and the convicts who were criminals, and that, although he was compelled by the duties of his office, to number us among the convicts, he was pleased to recognise that our convictions did not in any way affect our character as gentlemen.

Using then the discretion which was allowed him by the regulations, which defined the duties and the prerogatives of this position, he gave me a permit, written and signed with his own hand, by which I acquired the right to seek personally a job within the boundaries of the town of Sydney. I expressed to him, as best I could, my gratitude, and he invited me, with kindness and delightful politeness, to call and see him, now and again, at his office, so as to give him news of the success of my efforts. It would be difficult to express the joy with which I was filled, when leaving the office of this worthy man, my passport in my pocket and my heart full of hope. Now that I had partially recovered my freedom, it seemed to me that I had grown six inches. I blessed my benefactor, whose present and future happiness I committed to the protection of all the Saints of Paradise.

18

In Search of a Job

I had preserved, in the fold of the cover of my prayer book, a few gold coins brought out from Canada, and which, in this wise, had escaped the general confiscation effected on board the *Buffalo*. To this store was added the few shillings salary which had been paid to me by the confectioners.

I went to board at the home of a man who occasionally had visited us at Long-Bottom. The reason why this Sydney colonist showed interest in us arose from the fact that he had formerly lived in Montreal, where he had learnt to speak French passably well. This memory of Canada, which had led him to visit us, was the means which led me to take lodgings with his family.

Worthy Captain McLean had given me good advice, and had warned me that I would find many difficulties in finding employment in Sydney. He had informed me of the great economic depression which paralysed business, and had explained to me the causes of it. The fact is that at this time the whole Colony was in the throes of a shocking financial crisis; general bankruptcy was threatening people, and each day was marked by the announcement of more or less considerable failures.

The causes of this crisis were a result of the method of colonization, adopted four or five years previously by the Government, and of the fever of speculation which, consequently, had obsessed the population overcome with greed, and the thirst for material pleasures; for there were scarcely any who cared for religion.

Right up to the time that I have just mentioned, the English Government gave land, often in considerable lots, to all the colonists who were British subjects, and to emancipated convicts. In addition, England expended considerable amounts of money on the colony, and the penal administrators for the settlers supplied much cheap labour in the person of the convicts still carrying out their sentence. Besides this, the great work of road construction and the tasks round the seaports were carried out by the convicts, rationed, maintained and controlled by the government of the Mother Country.

This abundance of property thus reaching the settlers, in the form of free land grants and cheap hand-labour, in a word, of assistance of every kind, issuing from the English Treasury, brought rapid development to these far-distant settlements. A goodly number of people made magnificent fortunes. The report of these successes spread throughout the three kingdoms, and the tide of emigrants began to flow.

The English Government, seeing the value of the land increase, thought they should change the system of colonization. They began to sell the land by public auction, instead of granting it, and the produce of these sales was used to give free passages to all those who volunteered to emigrate.

This system, totally lacking in foresight, and in any charitable feeling, naturally produced disastrous effects. A mania for speculation took possession of the former settlers, who were already in possession of some capital; land values rose to prices which were entirely out of step with working conditions and markets. Not only was the country's capital thus exhausted; not only was future capital anticipated; but companies were promoted, which, by means of a certain amount of real capital obtained from England, and some fictitious capital locally subscribed, resulted in immense purchases of land and debts proportionately much greater still.

While this was happening in financial circles, the colony was inundated by waves of poor unfortunate immigrants. There was no work available amongst the former settlers for all this influx of people, thus suddenly transplanted into a world quite new to them. These fresh immigrants, on their part, had no means of purchasing land at the crazy prices that speculators had set up for it. All the floating capital had been absorbed by the purchase of land, and, instead of circulating within the colony, had passed entirely into the hands of the English ship-owners, who had transplanted to the southern lands these masses of immigrants who were entirely destitute.

Then began, at first, lack of means, then the money-lender, then the sacrifice of property, then bankruptcy. The speculators who, without even seeing them, had brought lands situated in the hearts of the bush, at the extravagant price of several pounds sterling per acre, were already unable to realize a single penny in ready money for excellent properties located in the neighbourhood of Sydney, even at tremendously reduced prices.

The distress was so great that the Government was compelled to have huts erected for the immigrants, and to feed these unfortunates for a somewhat lengthy time.

Such was the situation in New South Wales at the time when I left the office of the worthy Captain McLean, to look for a job in the town of Sydney. People in search of positions jostled one another in the streets and in the shops: merchants and manufacturers were beset by more job hunters than customers.

For a fortnight I went about knocking at doors and knocking at hearts, colliding everywhere with needy competitors, without being able to find the slightest thing to do. At first I had sought some sort of employment that was suitable to my tastes and skill, then I fell back on jobs less acceptable, and finally I was prepared to take the first that offered. But all was of no avail.

Meanwhile, my few gold coins and my few shillings had disappeared. At the end of three weeks my landlord, who was a bootmaker, and who also began to lack work, notified me that I could remain with him no longer. He had been paid, and he knew that I had exhausted all my resources.

Sydney from Flagstaff Hill, 1844.
The City of Sydney, from Lavender's Bay 1844, by John Skinner Prout.

19

I Become a Gardener

Before returning to a penal establishment I was determined to exhaust all possible avenues. I redoubled then my searches and solicitations, and this time, thanks to Providence, I had complete success. The job that I secured was that of assistant-gardener. My new master was a merchant-tailor, an emancipated convict who had grown rich during the colony's years of prosperity, and who had had the wisdom not to dissipate his wealth in the foolish speculations which had ruined so many others.

I went and informed Captain McLean of my good fortune, and furnished with the necessary papers signed by new master, I had myself, changed in due form from the service of my Frenchman from the Island of Mauritius to that of the Sydney merchant; for this formality was necessary to regularize my position. The conditions of the latter contract, for the hire of my person were the same as those of which I have already given an account. By my transferment from confectioner as I was, I had become gardener, and, in each of these instances, without serving any apprenticeship.

On the following day, I set out in a launch with my master's son, to go up the Parramatta River, on the banks of which the country property of the merchant was situated, about four miles from Sydney. It was a beautiful estate, of which at that time only eight acres were cleared of trees and cultivated as a garden. The working staff to which I had just been added, was composed of a chief gardener and five assigned prisoners.

The buildings were composed, first, of a country house, small but rather stylish, well-furnished and externally adorned with climbing plants; this was the cottage in which resided the owner's family during the course of their country excursions; second, a small dwelling which served as a home for the chief gardener and his family; third, another building occupied by the five assigned workmen.

My master's son, who was a very fine lad, showed me into the cottage occupied by the family, and pointing out to me an excellent bedroom which formed part of it, told me that his father had given him orders to place me in it, and to tell me, on his behalf, that he knew how to differentiate between the other convicts and myself, and that he intended that I should be respected and treated as an honest man, whom misfortune and not crime, had brought into this country. I thanked, most sincerely, my excellent companion, and I begged him to be good enough to offer to his father the expression of my profound gratitude for the consideration that he had for me. I assured him that I would endeavour to return that kindness by my punctuality at work, and my zeal for their interests. On his departure my young master recommended the head gardener to treat me well, and the assigned workmen to pay me due respect.

I was equally surprised and delighted with an action so sensitive and so generous. I was so much less prepared for it because such feelings were so alien to the behaviour of the people of this colony, at this period at least, and because certain newspapers, as I have already mentioned, had circulated regarding us the most infamous libels. However, at this period of our captivity, the prejudices stirred up against us began to die down, thanks to the influence of the Catholic clergy, and fair-minded men like Captain McLean and my new master, and thanks a little, too, to our good conduct.

Immediately after the departure of the owner's son, I provided myself with a pick and presented myself to the gardener. It was the season for pruning and manuring. As a farmer's son I was not wholly a stranger to these labours. I was, therefore, able to carry out my task to the satisfaction of my chief, who complimented me on my work.

The following day I was the first on the job, for I was determined to allow no one to get in ahead of me. I applied myself quickly to the task of gardening and clearing the land, and everything progressed as well as possible in our establishment. The excellent owner came now and again to visit his new property. He even came sometimes with his family. These visits were always holidays for us. For me he showed kindness and consideration even to the extent of including me in these rural gatherings of his family, and of offering me a glass of wine.

If I had not made it a rule in these notes to be brief, and not to allow myself to wander from the text, this fine conduct of a man who had risen from the convict class to that of honest and respectable citizen, would provide me with a subject suitable for a long digression, but with the limits I have set myself I must confine myself to mentioning his kindly action and to express the whole of the gratitude which I feel towards the honourable originator of it.

Three months after my arrival at the property of my new master all the Canadian prisoners were notified that they were to be removed from the category of "assigned convicts" (Ioues) to that of ticket-of-leave men (affranchis-surveilles). Having received this notice, we were to attend at the office indicated there to receive our permit or ticket-of-leave, which allowed us to work at whatever occupation we pleased, and on our own account, within the whole extent of the district mentioned on the ticket.

During the trip that I made to Sydney to get my ticket, I paid a visit to good Captain McLean and to my worthy estate owner. The latter told me that he was prepared to continue me in my present job, but that he would be happy to see me in possession of a better one. I then set to work to look for a better one, but things in the colony had not changed in any way, and it was impossible for me to find anything suitable.

From time to time I saw some of my companions in exile who were working in Sydney or its vicinity. One day when I met my friend Mr. Bourdon, he told me that the confectioners, in whose employ I had left him, had closed the shop, and that he had searched everywhere for a job but without success. He added that the only way he could conceive of being able to escape complete destitution was to rejoin ten of our compa-triots who had gone away to undertake a sawmilling job on the bushland belonging to a retired-soldier. He had decided to set out at once for the Canadian sawmill, and he urged me to follow him, pointing out to me that it meant almost complete freedom for us, and that thus reunited, it would be like a return to our own absent native land.

As this proposal had certainly its attractive side, I accepted. After having taken leave of my landowner, whom I thanked profusely for his good treatment of me, I spent some time with my good compan-ion, Mr. Bourdon, making, within the limits of our slender resources, the purchase of the necessary tools and provisions for one week. Having done this, with our sack upon our shoulders and the stick in our hand, we took the route that led to the Canadian Sawmill, through the bush, which we had been told was full of snakes and of enormous lizards, caned in that country, goannas.

Emigrants to Australia, housed in a Sydney warehouse during the financial dramas of 1844.

20

The Canadian Sawmill

The Canadian sawmill was only nine miles from Sydney on the opposite side of the Parramatta River and three miles from the river's bank. It was dense bush, but a well-defined track led to it, so we had no difficulty in following it.

From the information received, Mr. Bourdon and I had decided to set about making laths and we had set up our stock of tools with this intention. The reasons which had induced us to choose laths as the object of our manufacture were, first, because this did not necessitate contact with our comrades at the sawmill, who were occupied exclusively preparing carpenter's timber and sawn timber; second, because for this conversion of forest wood the work required less acquaintance with forestry work in general.

Having left Sydney in the morning, we crossed the river, and about noon reached the sawmill, where very soon our friends, who were highly delighted to see us, returned from their work for dinner. Our hosts for the moment were quartered in a spacious hut, built of wooden slabs, covered with the bark of trees. All around, as in the Canadian sawmills, were distributed rows of bunks, softly and plentifully stuffed with fern leaves and supplied with woollen blankets.

We prepared dinner with them, and during this time and the duration of the meal, we communicated to our compatriots our scheme whereby we should join them in the manufacturing of laths. Knowing that we were not accustomed to bush work, they expressed certain doubts about the definite results of our enterprise, but, at last they said, as there was nothing else to do in this wretched country, we must try anything at all. They volunteered to lend us a hand in the establishment of our enterprise.

None of us had time to waste. Continual hard work and strict economy were indispensable at that period in New South Wales. One could not get through otherwise. Consequently, as soon as dinner and the little round of conversation which was like dessert to it, were over, off we went to begin work. It was about one o'clock in the afternoon when we commenced our job, our ten friends directing and helping us.

An enormous tree, at least six feet in diameter at the base and more than a hundred feet high, was cut down and split into billets each four feet long, which was the length required for our laths. Our friends, who had assisted us in this first operation, taught us then the best method of splitting these billets and converting them into laths, after which they went off to resume their own work for the remainder of the day.

There still remained to us about two hour's working time, which Mr. Bourdon and I used, as well as we could, by continuing the same labours. During these two hours' work we each split about forty laths; in the same period of time a man highly skilled in this occupation would have split almost two hundred.

In the evening assembled the whole dozen of us in our hut, after our supper. We spent the most agreeable evening which so far it had been our lot to pass in the land of Australia. Until eleven o'clock, our conversation, mingled with Canadian songs, centred round our own dear country, our relatives and our absent friends. Each one of us thought and talked about his family, his parents, expressing the hope of seeing still once again, both of these before his death. This very pleasant conversation, doubtless, was not without grief, however, for there were amongst us husbands and fathers whose wives and children were absent and perhaps in necessitous circumstances.

Our work went on continuously, and we acquired experience and dexterity in our new handiwork, which, nevertheless, considerably tired my comrade, Mr. Bourdon, who was physically weak. Although more robust than my friend, neither did I fail to find the work very hard indeed; from the very first days we had our hands covered with blisters and our limbs stiff with fatigue.

After a week's work we had to go to Sydney to get some provisions. There we met the three principal officers of a French whaling ship from the port of Brest. They were returning from a whale-fishing cruise, made into the regions of the extreme South Pacific. We talked together about Old and New France; then, at their earnest entreaties, we told them the tale of our struggles and our misfortunes. Overcome by an intense sympathy for us, and moved by this feeling so peculiarly French, namely, devotion, they immediately offered to procure our escape from exile by taking us on board their ship. We thanked them warmly for their generous offer, but we told them that the thing was almost impossible, and made them understand the serious consequences which might result from it for them personally, for the laws in force against captains, officers and sailors of a vessel which gave refuge to a convict are extremely severe. The personal penalty is a fine of £500 sterling or imprisonment, and, in the case where the captain or the owners of the vessel are the authors of the attempt, then the penalty involved is confiscation of the ship herself.

In that case, said one of the officers, the doctor of the whaler, I'll take the whole responsibility; if we fail, I'll get out of it at the cost of a short term of imprisonment, and, in any case, the ship will be exempt from seizure. He was so persistent, and the prospect of being free so attractive, that we agreed to accept the generous doctor's proposal. He arranged everything in such a way as to compromise neither the captain nor the ship. He was to hide us in his pharmacy, of which he alone held the keys, and which was, at it were, his own private quarters, and for the administration of which he alone had the privilege and the responsibility.

It was two days later that the departure of the whaling vessel was due to take place. During the night which succeeded this preliminary arrangement, I began to think hard, and during the long period of sleeplessness brought about by the gravity of the situation, I weighed all the pros and cons. The result of my deliberations thus made by myself alone, was that it was far better not to attmept this adventure, so fraught with danger for the generous-hearted men who were so anxious to take part in it on our particular behalf, and for ourselves, too. Besides, in the case of complete success, I could see nothing better in the final result, than the obligation to live and to die outside of my native land.

I communicated to my friend, Mr. Bourdon, the result of my meditations, and my determination not to go away, which was the practical result of them. I told him that there was every reason to hope for a general pardon, and that, in these circumstances, our escape would be equivalent to perpetual banishment.

Mr. Bourdon told me that he was a husband and a father, that by taking advantage of the opportunity which was so generously provided by the officers of the French whaler, he would be able to go away to the United States, and send for his family; that in the event of a general pardon he would endeavour to have himself admitted to participation therein. In a word, he told me that he had made up his mind to leave.

He departed, in fact, with the whaler, which set sail the following morning, carrying away with her my comrade and my friend. Mr. Bourdon has given an account of his voyage in a work published several years ago. This companion of my misfortunes died last year; but at least he died upon the soil of his home land, and the country of his birth has been the repository of his ashes, within the shadow of the Cross of a Canadian cemetery.

I had to discover a fresh partner, for two persons were needed for our particular job. In the state of affairs then existing in_Sydney, I had no difficulty in discovering him amongst the Canadian exiles. He was Mr. Louis Ducharme.[16] On the same day as my friend, Mr. Bourdon, set sail, and when we had seen the ship which was bearing him away leave port, with our sack of provisions on our back, we took the bush road which led to our mill.

Valiantly we set to work, and disregarding our difficulties, our mistakes and our fatigue, we split laths from morning until night. Finally, in the course of two weeks, after our return to the mill, we had completed a cargo of 12,000 laths. First we engaged some carters to transport our wood to the river; then we hired a flat-bottomed boat to carry it to Sydney, where we effected the sale of it at the price of ten shillings sterling per thousand. That is to say, that we had in all just sufficient money to pay for the cutting of the wood, the carter, the hire of the barge, and to purchase provisions for another fortnight. It was not a very brilliant result, but we lived in comparative happiness in our hut with our compatriots.

The day following our sale we returned to the bush by way of the river, rowing the flat-bottomed boat on which we had taken down our laths, and which we wished to take back to the landing stage in the bush. We then resumed our toil, with much more courage now that we had acquired a certain skill at the trade, and because, especially, we were henceforth inured to the work, so that we felt only that natural fatigue which makes evening rest so sweet, and a good night's sleep so restorative. And finally, had it not been for the heat and the mosquitoes which soon began to torment us, we should have believed ourselves happy enough, so far as one could be at least in our present circumstances.

As we did not hope very soon to quit our present way of living, and as, comparing job with job, our actual timber-getting was worth at the time, at any rate, as much as any other, we resolved to build an earthen oven, in the Canadian style, so that we might cook in it our communal bread. Hitherto our flour had been made into loaves baked beneath the ashes on a flat stone in the Australian fashion. We passed then from the damper to the bread loaf, and it was a red-letter day in our lives. Everywhere that four or five Canadians resided together, a little later, an earthen oven could be seen erected, and the local inhabitants used to remark to one another "there are Canadians here," when they noticed this domestic convenience, hitherto unknown in the rural districts of New South Wales.

Thus pleasantly passed three fresh weeks of our exile, during which, each working day, we had fashioned another boatload of laths, greater in quantity than the first lot. But tranquillity does not last forever, and happiness is not an inhabitant of this earth; I assure the reader that we found even less of it in Australia than elsewhere. In the particular day in question, we had loaded our barge with our laths, with the intention of leaving early the following morning for the Sydney market. The barge was anchored offshore ready to receive us in the morning. Bad luck, however, decreed that, during the night it should be dragged by the tide on to a large rock upon which it capsized at low tide, discharging into the river the greater part of its cargo.

What then, was our astonishment and our despair on arrival at the beach, to see our barge half-full of water and our load scattered over the river. My comrade, especially, was quite overcome by the sight, but it was necessary to make the best of things and to endeavour to recover from the wreckage as much as possible of the flotsam and jetsam of our possessions.

After having emptied the barge of the water that it contained, we set to work to gather, with two little dinghies which we had there, those of our laths that the tide had scattered throughout the night. It was lucky that these laths were tied up in bundles, each one containing one hundred laths, and that, at the time of our arrival, the tide which had just finished rising, had brought back to the starting point almost everything carried away by the preceding ebb. Altogether we got out of the affair with the loss of our time and some hundreds of laths. But it was decidedly a matter of some importance for us, without taking into consideration the fatigue and the wearisomeness of this unexpected work. After having employed the hours when the tide was favourable collecting our laths, we applied ourselves to the task of reloading them into the barge; these varied tasks were not completed until evening. We then put the barge in a safe position for the night.

Early the following morning we rowed towards Sydney, having the current of the incoming tide against us. There was then blowing one of those warm winds which, in this place, are regularly replaced the same day by strong, cold southerlies. We put all our strength into the oars so as to arrive at the Sydney Quay before the return of the southerly. Already we could see the trees gathering the dust rising on the roads; already we could feel the atmosphere getting chill again from the effect of the first gusts of this unpropitious wind; but we were not more than a few yards from the landing place; we redoubled our efforts. We were bathed in perspiration! Our exertions were of no avail, the wind was upon us; we went backwards. We were then compelled to tack about, and to allow ourselves to return towards the place from which we had set out; but, this time, without rowing: we had only to steer our vessel, which loaded over and above the sides, offered much resistance to the wind.

It was still a day of losses, and of new risks to be run. We managed to regain the landing stage where we cast anchor at seven o'clock on the Saturday evening. With dejected hearts we again took the road towards our hut; for we had no more food. Already for several days our comrades had been feeding us, and we had counted on not returning until the Monday, and then with sufficient provisions to repay those which we owed them and to sustain ourselves during another fortnight at least. We were no less well received, however, even though we brought nothing with us, and Sunday was spent, as every other that we passed in the bush, dividing out time between prayers, reading and conversation concerning our absent native land.

On Monday we set out once again for Sydney, the weather being the finest in the world. Our cargo, through having been immersed in the water of the Parramatta River, suffered a reduction in price of sixpence a thousand, to which in the sale that we made that same day, we were compelled to submit. The yield from our cargo put us in a position to pay all our debts, and to buy food sufficient for sixteen or eighteen days; but we were able to make no other purchases except those of two pairs of camel's hair cloth trousers, one for my partner, the other for myself.

Thus, then, our work, toilsome as it was, sufficed to provide us with food, but that was all. Very soon my partner was almost without clothes, and my wardrobe was hardly any better than his. However, I could still appear in Sydney in my garments, while there was an occasion when my poor partner was compelled to borrow from our comrades, whose work was more lucrative, certain articles of wearing apparel, including a shirt, for in hut attire, all we had was a woollen jerkin, and the only hat a red wood tam-o-shanter. It is hardly necessary to ask whether our skins were bronzed, exposed in this way to the Australian sun.

21

How By Accident I Became a Candle-Maker of Sorts

We had been employed for a year manufacturing laths when a disaster overtook our establishment, one which might have had terrible consequences on our position, for everything is relative in this world.

A bushfire, started some miles from our hut, was advancing towards us, driven on by the wind, when we received the warning it was not more than two miles from our dwelling. As soon as the alarm was given to us, we rushed straightaway to the hut; one section of our group devoted itself to saving from the hut our clothes and other effects, our supply of food and some few valuables. Besides the clothes we were wearing, and our laths, of which a cargo was ready to be despatched, my partner and I possessed only two woollen blankets. Those who had loaded themselves with their effects, my partner being amongst the number, ran with their bundles towards a deep gully, surrounded by bare rocks, at the bottom of which a stream ran. The remainder of our company stayed behind to try to save the fabricated wood, planks, pieces of timber, shingles and laths.

As for myself, I made for the heap of laths, and set to work to clear round about this heap a large circular space right down to the bare ground, of all the leaves and dry branches. As soon as I had rid this circle of all that would provide a hold for the conflagration, I prepared to set fire to the heap of leaves and branches I had accumulated right round my safety cordon. I intended to set this fire going only at the moment when the major forest fire reached us, so as not to risk making uselessly two outbreaks instead of one. I did not wait long; at first a muffled roar, then deep smoke announced the approach of the destructive element. At the moment when the first sparks became visible to me through the openings in the bush, I set fire to several parts of my heaps of dry leaves. In an instant I was enveloped in flames, which rushed in all directions, but all away from me. This fire, lit by my own hands, destroyed around my laths and my own person, in a few seconds all that could provide fuel for the advancing flames.

I remained, leaning upon my heap of laths, from which I saw pass by, in all his majesty, that person who bears the name of Bushfire.

You should have seen the flames ferreting out all the corners of the bush, to devour everything that it met there in the way of leaves dried by the sun, and little scraps of dead wood. The fire moved away as quickly as we had seen it approach us. When it had passed, I returned to the hut where, very soon afterwards, we all gathered together again to contemplate the ruins of our establishment. The hut was in ashes; in all truth, however, it was not a serious loss. Within a couple of days it was replaced by another, equally large and just as comfortable. But there were losses; a large part of the wood prepared by our comrades had been burnt; they had even lost some of their effects and provisions deposited in a little clearing, because the distance from the hut to the gully was considerable enough, but our friends had made important saves, and they could endure this minor disaster.

As for our two selves, we had lost nothing; the only things that we had to lose, our skins, our two blankets, and our laths, were safe.

I forgot to say, what the reader, besides, must have guessed, that none of us suffered any personal injury; one only suffered a temporary inconvenience which made him feel faint, through over-exposure to the smoke and the heat during the work of saving the cut timber.

My partner, for a while, found himself wholly disgusted with bush life and the trade of lath-manufacturer. We resolved, then, to look for another job. Our last load completed, we said goodbye to our companions, whom, on my part, I left most regretfully, and we set off, once again, down the Parramatta River for the Sydney lath depots.

The next day, after paying our rent and our debts out of the sale of our cargo, we once again found ourselves on the Sydney streets, looking for a fresh job. The task was no easier than it was the preceding year; distress still existed, and the government was always under the obligation of feeding a certain number of immigrants, who were without any means of earning their living. Mr. Ducharme and I were compelled to separate, so that, each on his own account, might search for a job, with greater chance of success.

After five days fruitless search, I met three Frenchmen who had recently arrived in the country with the intention of setting up there as manufacturers, having, as they told me, sufficient capital. They had decided to begin manufacturing candles. As they could not speak a single word of English, they engaged me as their interpreter and their business adviser. I could make myself easily understood in this language learnt in prison and during exile. But I did not set myself up with the Frenchmen as a speaker of pure French. I declare that I was as incapable of such an engagement as I was of practising what this word denotes.

My employees established their factory eight miles from Sydney, and four miles away from any dwelling, so that once again I found myself in the bush and in buildings which much resembled the hut of the Canadian timber mill. In my new job I was not given any manual work; my duty consisted of purchasing tallow on the Sydney market, and of effecting the sale of candles in the same place, contingent upon there being tallow to buy and candles to sell. If the returns were not remarkable, variety, at any rate, was not lacking.

Three times a week and on foot I made the trip between our factory and the town of Sydney, usually alone, sometimes accompanied by one of the partners. Things were not going very well; the greatest part of the capital of my employers was illusion on their own part, and fair promises on the part of others. They were not even perfectly acquainted with the industry that they had chosen.

Foreseeing that the establishment would not last and that I should finish up by not being paid, at the end of four months I resigned my situation, and well it was for me that I did, for the result was exactly as I had forseen.

22

In Turn Farm Hand and Salesman

For the fifth time, then, I saw myself on the road looking for a job. I was known to everyone on the Sydney highway; I stopped at almost every establishment, my swag on my back and my stick in hand, asking for a job. Everywhere I was received politely, but the reply invariably was that they had as much staff as they were able to pay for.

I must remark here that public opinion, if the term "opinion" can be given to prejudices and to the far-fetched and ill-founded opinions that are so often imposed on the public, public opinion had undergone a complete volte-face in respect of the Canadian exiles, and that is the reason why we were able, in spite of the extreme harshness of the times, to find employment, whereas the Government was obliged to house and feed hundreds of immigrants, and a number of convicts returned perforce to the penal establishments.

I knew that my friend and former partner in the bush lath-making undertaking, Mr. Ducharme, was employed upon the land being cleared by one of the most comfortably-off men in Sydney. This citizen was a butcher who had amassed wealth in the course of the years of the colony's prosperity. I went and found him so as to ask him for work. Seeing that I was a Canadian, he replied at once that he would willingly employ me, but that, unfortunately, the only job he could offer me was working on his farm, where my compatriot was already engaged.

As there was no alternative, I at once accepted the offer, and the same day betook myself to the farm, situated in the neighbourhood of Sydney, where I found my friend pleased to see me rejoin him. We worked under the direction of a farm superintendent, and in agreement with him. When

I arrived at the property, Mr. Ducharme was living in a hut something like our dwelling at the timber mill. I took up my quarters with my friend.

We had been working two months on this farm when we met one Sunday at church our friends from the Canadian timber mill. They had given up their timber-getting business because sales were no longer profitable; for hitherto their trade in sawn timber, boards and shingles had been very profitable for them. In the whole Colony they were, undoubtedly the most capable and the most skilful in this variety of work; but the fact is that, in consequence of the excessive number of unemployed, and the exhaustion of capital, all industries, one after another, were collapsing.

Two of our former companions at the sawmill, Mr. J. M. Thibert and Mr. F. X. Touchette, who had accumulated a little money, proposed that I should join them in operating a business proposal that they had formulated, on advice and information that had been supplied to them. My two friends, of whom one was a farmer and the other a blacksmith, offered to provide the small amount of capital necessary at the start, and only required that I should put at the service of the partnership my business knowledge.

About twelve miles from Sydney, on the road which was then the most frequented in the colony, there were the beginnings of a village which had already been christened with the name of Irish Town, although this *ville irlandaise* was still composed of only two public houses and three colonists huts; it was there that we set up our place of operations.

Our venture was projected with the idea of making customers out of the travellers passing along the road, and with that intention, we wished to be able to offer them articles of which they might often have real need while on the road. The establishment was to comprise a small shop selling foodstuffs and groceries, a bakery and a blacksmith's shop.

Those who, in our country have had the opportunity of visiting the establishments of new settlements far distant from centres or villages of some importance, have, doubtless, sometimes noticed displayed in the little shop windows of a settler's hut some twists of tobacco, pipes, small bottles containing pepper, cinnamon, nutmegs, cream candy bars for children, etc., etc. These examples may give a fairly correct idea of the type of business that, at the time of which I speak, our three compatriots only recently arrived in New South Wales, were about to establish.

The bush was not very far away from the "town" of Irish Town, so we had very little difficulty in finding material for our premises. Big slabs or wooden posts were prepared by us; then we collected sheets of bark, the whole of which were dragged to the site of our future business by a quiet working bullock hired for the occasion. Six days after our arrival three buildings, a grocer's shop, a bakery and a blacksmith's forge, had been added to those of which Irish Town was already proud.

Our oven, built of potter's clay in the Canadian style, which is the best, as we have taken the opportunity of asserting, was located near to the hut where we proposed to knead our dough and to make it rise.

For many of the settlers passing along the road, the construction of this oven was an object of extraordinary curiosity, which was of value to us as a good advertisement. You should have heard the remarks of which this structure was the object on the part of those who, in large numbers, stopped to watch us at work. What interested them most was the timber framework upon which we were building the clay arch of the oven.

It was a true study of the human mind to listen to the conversations which took place amongst our visitors. Some had the good sense and the good taste to confess that they understood nothing at all about it, and to ask for explanations, which we gave with pleasure, at the same time begging them to say nothing about it to the others so that we could derive some amusement from the remarks of each; others who did not in the least understand what we were doing set themselves up as experts, and naturally without giving the least explanation, said that it was simple to understand, and finally others with that gross conceit so well-known, said, "These Canadians then must be very stupid if they imagine that they are going to heat this oven without burning the timber of which it is built, and consequently without its collapsing. Circumstances such as these gave rise to an infinitely greater display of lack of education and foolish pride than of wise reticence and humble search for knowledge, which accompany honest common sense and a good domestic education.

Curiosity to see our oven heated, and then to eat good homemade bread that was baked in it, from the very first attracted to us a fairly good lot of customers, and we had much hearty fun at the expense of those foolish dolts who imagined that we were going to bake bread in a wooden oven. It was a fellow countryman who came and instructed us in the baking trade, and my comrade, Mr. Thibert served an apprenticeship of two days, which sufficed to teach him to make bread superior to all the dampers of the rural settlers in the colony. As a matter of fact the bakery was the only thing that brought us in a little profit. The shop yielded very little and the blacksmith's forge practically nothing at all. So, after a month's trial, our comrade, Mr. Touchette, who was bent on carrying on his trade as a blacksmith, left us to go and set up about five miles distant, where he did a larger amount of business. This separation was in the interest of all of us; our friend was able to gain his living in his new premises, and two of us remained to share all the income that our trading could provide. Our profits were not enormous, but they were sufficient for our food and our upkeep, and we lived peacefully and in almost complete freedom to the degree that we would almost have considered ourselves free men in a foreign land had it not been for our obligation to report once a month at the ticket-of-leave office. Our peaceful life at Irish Town was not distinguished by any remarkable incident, except possibly one. My companion and myself, I believe I shall be able to say so without boasting, constituted at once the aristocracy of birth, of intellect and of wealth in the town where we were dwelling; as regards titles and symbols of nobility I am of the opinion that we were all on the same level on the Empire's Registers, that is all convicts carrying tickets of leave. We were believed to possess some money, and we slept, my comrade in the bakery and I in the shop, two small buildings alongside one another. During one dark night I was awakened by a strange noise, which I immediately suspected to be caused by robbers. I jumped out of my bed, calling for my mate at the top of my voice, which put the thieves to flight, for such they were. We were just in time, since we found the chest which contained our belongings and the little capital of our business upon the doorstep where the robbers had abandoned it. Thus ended an incident which might have proved a minor disaster for us, if not a greater misfortune, for, in a country such as this, housebreakings are very often accompanied or followed by bloodshed.

23

The First Pardons and the First Returns Home

We had been residing almost a year at Irish Town when the news arrived that two of our companions in exile, Mr. Charles Huot and Mr. Louis Pinsonneault, had been pardoned. It was quite an event for the exiled Canadians, all scattered throughout Sydney and its surroundings; for each of us it was the presage and a foretaste of the end of our exile, a commencement of the carrying out of the prayers and the promises of our friends in Canada, and of the prediction of the worthy officer whom we had met in Hobart-town.

On learning this news, I set out immediately to pay a visit to myoid friend, Mr. Huot, so as to be more certain of the truth of the report that had been made to us. Mr. Huot resided in the immediate vicinity of Sydney. He was at home and he showed me the document he had received. For some considerable time I held in my hand this piece of paper, and several times read over this statement, which restores freedom to convicts.

The joy which this pardon, so eagerly desired, brought to Mr. Huot was, for the moment, particularly modified by a feeling of sadness, the cause of which I had little difficulty in guessing. My respected friend had not sufficient means to take advantage of this pardon and to pay the expenses of his return home. For us freedom was of little consequence without a return home; for, slaves or freemen, convicts or pardoned, New South Wales and every other land except that of Canada, was exile for us.

Everyone probably knows that we, just like all other Australian exiles, had ourselves to provide our own return fares as far as England. Generous subscriptions made in our country districts and in our towns to provide for the expenses of our voyage were deposited in England, and it was necessary for us to go there to obtain assistance out of this fund, which had been, however, sufficient to charter a good stout ship, stored with everything necessary to convey us all from Sydney to Quebec. For the majority of us this was a source of anxiety, disappointment, delays and unbelieveable efforts.

After having congratulated my good old friend on his good fortune, and having consoled him in his sadness, by encouraging in him the hope that Providence would provide the means of restoring him to his homeland, I again returned to Irish Town, turning over in my mind thoughts of hope and doubt about our future in connexion with those who were not, apparently, included in this first act of pardon. "Why should there be this differentiation?" I wondered. Why should the determination thus have been made to limit the Royal clemency? Then I put to myself all sorts of questions, that the reader, inferentially, can imagine, concerning the explanation of the whole affair.

When I arrived at our own dwelling, I announced to my partner the confirmation of the news, which he was awaiting with great anxiety. As pleased as myself with the good fortune of our two companions in misfortune, he was infinitely more distressed than I with the various ways that fate struck at us; it was perfectly natural, for he was a husband and the father of a young family who were grieving at his absence.

A month later, the mail-boat, which every month brought the English mail, brought this time the pardons of more than half of the Canadian exiles, among which was my pardon. This news overwhelmed us all with delight, for it was a certainty for some and a sign of hope for the others. The reader knows that this hope did not prove false for anyone of us.

Nothing on earth, I am sincerely of the opinion, could have persuaded us to remain far away from our own native land; neither wealth nor distinctions. We were a-hungered and a-thirst for our homeland, we were consumed with the desire to return to Canada, to see again our families, our friends, our beautiful countryside, to salute the belfries of our parishes, to speak French, and to gaze on the sight of our good Canadian-French customs.

The majority of the Canadian exiles had, fortunately, been able despite the stress of the times, to accumulate some savings sufficient to provide for the expenses of their return, and my partner was amongst this number, but, unfortunately, the others had no means whatsoever, or means that were quite insufficient, and I was amongst this latter number.

It was necessary for us, Mr. Thibert, who was departing; and for myself, who was remaining, to wind up the affairs of our little business venture. This business had provided us with a comparatively comfortable living; in addition, it entirely saved my partner from encroaching upon his savings made in the saw-mill business and other little industrial under-takings, and set aside to pay for his return home. He had given me the means of restoring my wardrobe, but apart from that, when our debts were paid, there remained to the partnership only its buildings and its oven, which no one wanted, and which were not worth the trouble of being offered up for sale.

Once more I found myself on the Sydney streets in search of a job. I have already said that the better we Canadians became known, and con-sequently when the effects of the newspaper slanders and the antipathy created by the prejudices of race and religion so deeply rooted in the pop-ulation began to disappear, we obtained employment much more easily. At the period of which I speak, we were even commencing to become the object of marked preferences; so I had no difficulty this time in finding a position, and under conditions and with a salary much superior to any to which I might have dared aspire previously. I took up duty as a clerk with one of the principal dry goods warehouses in Sydney.

During this same period, twenty-eight of my companions liberated from bondage were engaged making preparations for their departure. It was the month of August, 1844. They had joined forces to negotiate con-cerning the price of their passages as far as England with the captain of a merchantman about to depart. It was the best available means, and they succeeded in making a good bargain. I had not been in place behind my new master's counter more than four days than they came to say goodbye to me, and to wish me, personally, an equally prompt departure. I gave them my best wishes for a happy return to the homeland: my feelings betrayed the profound distress that I felt at not being able to accompany them. They cheered me up, telling me that our fellow citizens would not abandon us ; that a subscription would certainly be taken up to take us back from these shores whose soil would almost scorch my feet until I was permitted again to see our beloved Canada.

That same evening, several of us gathered together again to console one another a little, and for mutual encouragement, founding our hope for a speedy departure upon a thousand more or less probably hypotheses. We relied upon the generosity of our compatriots, and we did not rely in vain; but I do not know how it happened that the persons entrusted with the administration of the relief funds could not then find the means of transmitting this money to us at once, since it was of more use to us in Sydney than in England.

Thirty-nine of our compatriots, including Mr. Bourdon, had left the land of exile; two had died there; seventeen were remaining there still, when I made the acquaintance in Sydney of a French merchant, who, disgusted with the country, and seeing no probability of improvement in the affairs of the colony, had made up his mind to sell at any price the considerable stock-in-trade of latest fashion articles which remained to him from his importations from France.

Mr. Philemon Mesnier, such was the name of this merchant, often spoke to me of my country and of my misfortunes and each time I answered him in terms of a tone of voice which made him understand the intense fierceness of the desire which was consuming me to see again my homeland.

Homesickness preyed upon me, and this disease threatened to bring me to the grave. Never, at any period of my exile, had I experienced anything approaching it. The boredom that I suffered is indescribable; it pursued me everywhere. I was very soon on the verge of falling into a state of melancholia, and of seeking only solitude, in the depths of which I nourished my sorrow. Every Sunday I spent the afternoon on a rock situated in the recesses of a solitary little bay overlooking Sydney Harbour; there I dreamed over my homeland and my family. It seemed to me that my eyes were watching the wake of the ship which had carried away my lucky comrades. My thoughts accompanied this ship; with it I ranged the seas; with it I reascended the St. Lawrence; then the picture of the parish where I was born; then my mother's kisses, the joy of my old father, the hand-clasps of my friends passed through my mind, only to surrender me very soon to the harsh reality which made me find myself once again upon the wretched rock of the land of my exile. Then I was overcome by the anguish of unhappiness, during which I cried out ceaselessly, "When, oh when, shall I be able to set out for Canada?"

YOUNG CANADA
DELIGHTED WITH RESPONSIBLE GOVERNMENT.

24

A Generous Soul

The worthy French merchant had noticed the weakness which was sapping my strength, and had taken compassion on me; he suggested taking me into his service to help him wind up his affairs, after which, before leaving for Europe, he promised to take me away with him, and to provide me, should I need them, with the means of returning to Canada. After having obtained from my employer at that time permission to leave his service, I accepted Mr. Mesnier's offer, which was for me a real cure. Comforted by the prospect thus presented to me, I set to work with as much zeal as pleasure to assist Mr. Mesnier in the work of selling the stock in his warehouse.

At this date we had all been pardoned, but seventeen of us were still in Sydney, detained in exile through lack of funds. Every Sunday, and sometimes in the evenings, we met to console one another, to talk about our homeland, and to exchange our reasons for hoping for an early release.

Now and again there departed one of us who had succeeded in getting together the price of his passage-money to England; three of the seventeen of whom I have spoken preceded me over the ocean tracks which lead to Canada.

About ten months had rolled away since the departure of the thirty-eight whom I mentioned, when one fine day, one of the messengers from the home of the Governor, Sir George Gipps, came and informed me that His Excellency wished to see me. As I had nothing to fear, in the future, I surmised that some good news was awaiting me, and it was with a heart full of hope that I set to work to smarten myself up so as to present myself before the representative of the Sovereign.

His Excellency received me with kindness and politeness; he even appeared to be interested when he saw and talked with me. He disclosed to me then the contents of a letter he had received which informed him that several members of the parishes had requested Her Majesty's Government to. be so good as to undertake the responsibility of transmitting and distributing to the Canadian political prisoners a considerable sum of money, the result of a subscription taken up iii Canada, with the aim of providing for the expenses of our return home. Sir George added that nothing had yet been done since the departure of the mail boat, but that, whereas it was probable that the next mail boat would bring him the order and the funds to send us all back to England, he had believed it his duty to send for me so as to forewarn me and to ask me to advise my comrades to hold themselves in readiness.

I thanked His Excellency for this consideration, as much on my own behalf as in the names of all my companions still in exile in Sydney, after which, offering to His Excellency my most courteous good wishes, I hastened to make my way speedily to the homes of all my comrades and friends to share with them the happy news that I had just learnt, and from a source as valuable as it was authentic.

Nevertheless, for some considerable time still we did not get beyond the transports of joy into which this piece of news had thrown us. The mail boats kept on arriving every month, one after another, and nothing came for us. However, we did not lose hope; we knew quite well that the Governor had not been joking at our expense and we well believed him to be almost as disappointed as we were at having thus induced to shine in our eyes a hope which was not realized. Besides, in all that, there was one thing that appeared to us quite certain, and that was that a sufficient subscription had been taken up by our compatriots, and that the total amount of this had been deposited in England. Then we said to one another, "Be brave, sooner or later it must come."

A good number of those who remained were in a state bordering on distress and did not see how, then or ever, they would be able to accumulate the sum considerable enough needed to pay for a passage from Sydney to England. One alone amongst them was a sailor[17] but he was an old man, but no ship's master was anxious to add to his crew men who would suffer from sea sickness with every storm that blew. Besides there were so many young men with good sea-legs who sought in this way to earn their return to Europe that the captains were able to accept men already accustomed to salt water.

As for myself in particular, except for exile and the home sickness which it caused me, I was best off in the house of my generous employer. To the excellent material delights of comfortable circumstances were added in my case the still more precious delights of the most cordial sympathy and of the most delicate and disinterested friendship. I was sometimes a little perturbed, so much was I afraid by some indiscretion, of trespassing on so liberal and so outstanding a hospitality.

Towards the end of January, 1846, that is to say, about eighteen months after the first departure of the Canadian exiles, on their return to Canada, my excellent employer wound up all his affairs. Everything was liquidated. He had completed the sale of the rest of his goods and had realized the whole of his possessions, not, however, without making great sacrifices. But he was in almost as much haste to leave these Australian shores as I was.

He set out, then, and I accompanied and helped him, as one can well imagine, in quest of a ship about to sail. There wer e several which announced their departure during the month of February. We visited them all, and after having obtained information regarding their sea-going qualities, we selected as the most comfortable and the finest sailer, the ship *Saint George*, commanded by a Captain Jones. There is no need to say that the *Saint George* had not the least" resemblance to the *Buffalo*, whose fate, however, at the present time, I should love to know.

A wounded man preserves as a memento the bullet or the piece of shrapnel that has been extracted from his lacerated flesh. Well, I, too, would like to possess a little cross made from the wood from which this vessel was constructed, and within whose sides my heart and my body have been lacerated by unworthy treatment.

25

The Return Voyage

On Shrove Sunday of the month of February 1846, in the morning, after having taken farewell during the preceding days of the kindly disposed persons to whom I was under obligations, and of whom I have spoken in the course of this narrative, I embarked, in the company of Mr. Mesnier, my benefactor, Mrs. Mesnier, his worthy spouse, and a fairly large number of other passengers, on board the *Saint George*, bound for England.

Several of the thirteen Canadian exiles who remained behind in the land of exile, had been able to accompany me on to the wharf. They shook my hands, wishing me a happy return home. They were greatly moved, and I in tears, saying to them, "Be brave, my friends, be brave, your turn will come!"

Some of my fellow-travellers, almost all people who were abandoning the colony as a result of their abortive attempts to prosper, shared our emotion; .others looked as though they deserved to remain instead of my brave comrades.

The *Saint George*, at eleven o'clock, raised her anchor, and, with sails outspread, commenced her long course of thousands of miles across the mighty waters of the deep. The weather was magnificent; a light breeze filled our sails; the noble vessel glided majestically over the waves, steering her way towards the mouth of the harbour.

With what great pleasure I saw the shores of New South Wales vanish in the distance, and had it not been for the sadness caused by the thought of my poor companions remaining in Sydney, I believe that at this moment I would have been as happy as anyone in the world. It seemed to me that already I was prepared for my arrival home. I seemed to hear my parents saying to one another, "At last, here he is!" and asking themselves, "Has exile much changed him?" Already I saw myself at the domestic fireside surrounded by relatives and friends to whom I told the story of my long sufferings. Already I saw all my acquaintances gathering round me on Sunday on the church steps, as we came out of the parish mass. Oh, image of my native land, how I have pictured you from all the degrees of latitude and longitude which separate Canada from the land of Australia.

For several days we were favoured with a stern wind, accompanied by fine weather. We made our way in the most pleasant manner in the world, steering for Cape Horn. I followed, consequently, a route wholly different from that by which we had come to Sydney on board the *Buffalo*, upon which ship we had doubled the Cape of Good Hope.

After two weeks of the most delightful travelling, during which Mr. Mesnier and I talked ceaselessly about old and new France, that is when Mrs. Mesnier was not speaking to me of my parents, and especially of my mother, we were in the latitude of New Zealand. There, for some days, we experienced adverse winds accompanied by squalls; but soon the fair wind returned and we resumed our swift course towards the cold, wet regions round Cape Horn.

Having reached the latitude of Cape Horn, we were overtaken by a complete calm, which lasted for a whole week. The spectacle to be seen all round was one of magnificent gloom, and the calm seemed to bring with it terrors which never accompany storms. It grew cold, very cold; the ship was surrounded by great ice-bergs; the sky was so dark as to necessitate the use of lights in full daytime; thick clouds stretched like dismal, weeping veils, and seemed to descend as low as the tops of the masts of our ship. The fog soaked the deck and the rigging, and this water formed an icy crust upon the deck, and hung in crystals from the rigging. The calm which kept us back seemed, in a word, to carry torment in its breast.

At the end of this week of calm, a violent north-west wind arose, by the help of which we doubled the Cape; but steering towards the south as far as the vicinity of a little island called, I believe, Royal Island, where we encountered once again the calm, which this time lasted for only one day.

During the night of the same day, a gusty wind, blowing from the south east, in four or five days, sent us into the neighbourhood of the St.

Malo Islands. There, so it appears, we were in imminent danger. The wind drove us towards the coast, and during almost the whole day we coasted the shores of one of these islands, having all the trouble in the world to prevent the ship being driven on the rocks that we could see from the level of the deck. Finally, towards evening, the wind abated somewhat, then turned in a more favourable direction, and we were able, changing our course a little, to move away from this dangerous locality. The following day the breeze was entirely favourable, and we made good progress, travelling north east at full speed.

Ten days had passed since we had escaped from the dangers of the reefs surrounding the Islands of St. Malo; the ship was bowed beneath the strain of a strong wind, and the sea beat furiously against its frail outer timbers. It was four o'clock in the afternoon and we were seated at table; a noise was heard up on deck; then we heard the order to bring the vessel to. The minute after the ship underwent a change of course, accompanied by a heavy sea, which made her tremble throughout her whole framework.

The order to bring the vessel to had been given by the third officer on board, then in charge of the ship. The captain and the second officer, at table with us, upsetting everything in their way, rushed up on to the quarter deck to find out the cause of so unexpected a manoeuvre, and to take charge of things. They were followed closely by all the passengers, who rushed in confusion on to the deck, asking anxiously, "Have we struck a rock? Is it a collision? Are we going to perish?"

On the ship everything was in a state of confusion, and we found the crew in this terrible emergency terror-stricken, preparing to launch the ship's boats. Doubtless it was a disaster of which no one knows or can perceive the cause. The majority of the passengers were already rushing into the boats, and some dreadful drowning incidents were just about to be recorded when the captain succeeded in securing the attention of these fear-stricken wretches. He explained to them then that the cause of these manoeuvres was the falling overboard of an unfortunate sailor. He begged everyone to withdraw into the stern of the ship, to permit the crew to work at one moment, the ship readily, and to carry out unhindered the dangerous life-saving operations in the midst of a rough sea, whipped by a heavy storm wind.

Leaning on the hand rail of the ship I could see the unfortunate sailor struggling with the waves; for about ten minutes I watched him appear and disappear turn about; he was visible on the crest of a wave; at another he seemed to have been engulfed beneath its trough. It was a sight to chill the heart.

A ship's boat was launched by five sailors. It made its way towards the poor fellow, at this moment the plaything of the waves. How anxiously we followed the movements of this frail craft, buffeted by the sea, advancing with difficulty despite the exertions of the powerful rowers. At last the boat approached the poor sailor. We felt almost choking with impatience awaiting the moment when, gripped by one of his comrades, we should see him snatched from the terrible fate which awaited him. The boat was not more than a few yards from him when we saw him disappear beneath the waves. The boat's crew searched for some time, scanning the rough surface of the sea, then turned back towards the side of the ship, on a signal to return given by the captain's order. I felt my chest oppressed as though by a heavy weight. Now I feared for the fate of the five men who comprised the crew of the flimsy little boat. Actually they had great difficulty in returning, but at last they got back. The ship resumed its course, each person went back to his usual occupation on board, and an hour later no one would have perceived that an accident had just taken place on the vessel which was taking us across the tracks of the ocean. There are so many of these poor children of Adam who, any day, at any hour, at any minute pass from time to eternity, from the judgment of men often so false, to the infallible and terrible judgment of God!

Each day's advance during March left the cold southern regions farther and farther behind us and brought us nearer and nearer to the heat of the torrid zone. After two and a half month's travel we came into port at Pernambuco, in South America.

The heat there was intense, but passing through these attitudes how I again revelled in the difference existing between my position on the *Saint George* and that which I occupied on board the unforgettable *Buffalo*. Then a slave, today I was a free man; then despised, now I was respected; heading the exiles' road then, now I was returning home; and from the merely physical side, instead of the filth of the frigate, I had all the comfort that can be enjoyed on board a passenger ship.

As the captain had business on shore, we, that is Mr. Mesnier, his wife, some passenger and myself took the advantage of this to go and breathe for a while the fresh air of the fields and the woods so rich in the natural products of warm countries. I do not give a description of the little town and harbour of Pernambuco; such a description would resemble a thousand others of the same kind, and would not have any great interest for my readers.

Having gone ashore about eleven o'clock in the morning, we did not return to the ship until about nine o'clock in the evening. To get back, eight of us went on board a boat rowed by native oarsmen. As they rowed they sang a lament on a Spanish song, the air of which was wonderfully sweet, and had as its refrain, "Santa Maria!" They had not repeated this refrain twice, the sound of which caused me great pleasure, than I joined in the chorus which answered back; then Mrs. Mesnier joined in with us, then the whole eight of us repeated the sweet refrain, "Santa Maria !"

Once more back on the deck of our ship, I leaned my elbows upon the rail of the bulwarks, and remained there, drinking in the affecting melody of the oarsmen's song, until the very last "Santa Maria" that my ears could catch in the distance and brought back to me by the warm and gentle breezes of the tropics.

Next morning, about ten o'clock, the *Saint George*, and ourselves, one convoying the others, resumed our course towards the British Isles. After six weeks, from the day of our departure from Pernambuco, marked some-times by calm, at others by a favourable wind, we arrived at the London docks, all safe and sound, and in good fettle. We congratulated one another on our happy four month's trip, which allowed all of us to reach our destination ... all except our unfortunate sailor, to whose memory we paid the tribute of a few words.

26

In London

Everyone made haste to land. We, that is Mr. Mesnier, my protector, Mrs. Mesnier and I went ashore to an hotel with which my generous protector was acquainted. I poured out my thanks, offered from the depths of my heart, to my benefactor, and his noble wife, and offered them my services in London, if any of their business affairs should render such services desirable.

Mr. Mesnier had no need of me; but I still had several days of their pleasant company to enjoy. May God reward them for having restored to me my country, and for having, in this work of charity, performed such noble and such delicate actions.

On my arrival in London, as far as I, myself, was concerned, I had nothing more urgent than to discover the place where I could find the financial aid sent over from Canada for the return of the political exiles. I did not know where to go, or to whom to speak, in this immense confusion which is called London, where each person seems to be pursued by the demon of greed, and never to have a minute to devote to the next person. In this state of perplexity I resolved to approach Mr. Roebuck,[18] the distinguished member of the English House of Commons, whose zeal for Canadian interests was known to me. I went, therefore, to his office; but the person who was looking after it told me that Mr. Roebuck was away at Ham with his family. However he was expected back any day. It was on Wednesday that I went for the first time, to the office of the friend of the Canadians. I returned again the following day, and then on the Friday. Mr. Roebuck, not having yet returned on the Saturday, I adopted the course of writing to him to ask him for the information which at that moment I was so much in need.

On Monday morning I received a reply to my letter. Mr. Roebuck gave me all the necessary information; then he asked me a host of questions, full of sympathy and solicitude for my exiled companions still remaining in Australia. I hastened to reply to his friendly letter. I gave him the number of Canadian exiles retained in Sydney; I acquainted him with their unhappy condition, and the almost utter impossibility of their returning home for a long time by means of their own resources on account of the state of affairs in the colony, and lastly, I did my very best to increase, if possible, the interest he showed to my comrades and friends whom I had left so unhappy in New South Wales.

Mr. Roebuck had recommended me to Mr. Graham, indicating precisely where I would be able to meet this gentleman. I took a cab, and, accompanied by Mr. Mesnier, who continued to be helpful to me, I went to the street and the number indicated. Mr. Graham received me with the most cordial kindness, spoke to me words of congratulation upon my fortunate return from exile, and at once gave to me the sum of money necessary to pay for my passage as far as Montreal, and to defray the expenses of my stay in London.

When I returned to my hotel I found a second letter from Mr. Roebuck, who informed me that he could not come to London on account of family illness. He asked me some additional questions concerning the conditions under which my exiled companions were living. I replied immediately to this second letter, and expressed the hope of seeing him in London before my departure, at the approaching opening of Parliament, telling him that I had now two motives for so wishing, viz., that of the recovery of the sick member of his family, and also of having the happiness of seeing him and thanking him personally. This wish was not realized, however, as Mr. Roebuck did not return to London before my departure; but I received a third letter from him two hours before I left for Canada. He told me in this last letter that the sum deposited in England was not sufficient to accomplish the return to Canada of all the Canadians who remained in Australia. Not a single one of us, he added, should be compelled to remain in exile through lack of the pecuniary means of returning to his homeland. He asked me then to undertake the duty of making this fact known to my fellow-countrymen on my arrival in Canada, and to solicit fresh subscriptions.

Immediately following my interview with Mr. Graham, I had booked my passage on board a ship scheduled to depart on the 10th July. This ship was called the *Montreal*. From amongst all the ships about to sail for Canada, I had chosen the *Montreal* on account of her name. It seemed to me that this local name would bring me good luck.

I found very long these few days that I still had to spend in the gloomy English metropolis while waiting the departure of the ship which was to carry me towards the shores of the St. Lawrence, whose banks already seemed to smile at me. Of all the means of distraction that I tried, one alone, as it were, has remained in my memory, and that was my presence at a great military review, headed by the Duke of Wellington, in honour of the Viceroy of Egypt, then on a visit to the Court of Saint James. It was not a review as great as can be seen sometimes in France and in other military countries of Europe, but it is the most considerable I have ever seen, and it was a most imposing and most magnificent sight. I was enabled to witness the fanatical enthusiasm with which the English people were inspired for the person of the Duke, for there is no need to add his name of Wellington. There were, as ever, several Dukes in England at this time, but *he* was always *the Duke*. The troops were magnificent, and all the citizens of London, when they saw the Duke of Wellington pass by on his superb charger, surrounded by his staff, did not hesitate to place him above Alexander, Caesar, and especially Napoleon.

27

From London to Quebec

On the 13th July 1846, after a fortnight's stay in the heart of the immense metropolis of the United Kingdom, I left the London Docks on board the excellent ship *Montreal*, commanded by the pleasant, as well as skillful mariner, Captain Forbes. A steamer towed us out of the Thames and left us at some little distance from the shores of the English channel.

Scarcely had we arrived in this Channel which separates England from the Continent than a violent wind arose, which, alternating between calm and a redoubling in fury, kept us tacking about in the English Channel for three weeks. The *Saint George* had, in two days, traversed the space that we took about eighteen to clear. It is well-known that the swell and the waves of the English Channel are without equals in the whole extent of the oceans for the strain that they impose upon ships. These three weeks of stressful navigation had so shaken the structure of the *Montreal* that she began to leak. During the whole of the journey the crew, to its great annoyance, often expressed in English sailor's language, were compelled to man the pumps for several hours each day.

Our course across the ocean was, however, quite pleasant. The only distressing incident which happened was the death of a little child belonging to a very respectable emigrant family. The grief of these our fellow passengers aroused the sympathy of all on board. It is so sad to experience death and the burial which follows it at sea.

On the 2nd September, at seven o'clock in the morning, Oh, I remember it as though it were to-day, we saw, on going up on deck, the shores of the Gaspe district.

The Homeland! After more than seven years of exile. What emotions! It was something so sweet, so intoxicating that I began to say to myself:

"After all such rejoicings are not too dearly bought! If one experiences so much delight at returning to the soil of his homeland, what would not then be the joy of those who, after having proved worthy on earth, will be admitted to the delights of the Celestial land."

Thus did I dream, watching until I was tired out, the skies and the waters and the land of my native country. My delight appeared to all my travelling companions so great that they marvelled at it. One passenger, a former major in the English army, in his goodness of heart, was so affected by my happy state that he invited me to go down into his cabin, where, with the Captain, he had arranged a little party. They drank my health, and to Canada, so much beloved by her children, and congratulated me on my return to my ancestral hearth.

These feelings, so keen and so deep, produced upon me a peculiar effect such as nothing previously in my life, so fraught with incident during the nine years now passed, had been able to produce, with the result that for more than twice twenty-four hours I had no sleep.

From Gaspe, a week's journey between the two superb banks of the most beautiful river in the world, we came to the port of Quebec, where we cast anchor on the 10th September, which was a Sunday, about two o'clock in the afternoon. I went ashore immediately after our arrival, leaving on board my trunk, which, however, was not a very big one. I took a carriage on the spot, and was driven to a Canadian hotel. The tiniest things have their meaning in situations like these. I cannot express, for example, the effect that the sight of this carriage had upon me and the impression that I experienced when I heard French spoken around me, and noticed, especially, these simple words that the coachman addressed to his horse, "Gee-up now." A thought flashed through my mind. The picture of Long-Bottom appeared mentally in contrast. I seemed to hear, in opposition to the words of command that my coachman addressed to his Canadian horse the words so coarse in our tongue and to our ears that we used towards our associates in hand labour, the Australian bullocks, "Hi! Dji!" It is thus, in order to confound and humiliate us that God allows these trivial ideas to run through our poor brains often in the most solemn moments. Who is there who has not experienced that several times in his life?

28

Home at Last

I do not know who spread the news that a Canadian exile had just arrived from Australia, but every minute I received a visit from some citizen of Quebec (where I hardly knew anyone) who came and congratulated me on my return, wished me welcome and asked me for news of our compatriots still remaining in exile. They did not know what to do to give me pleasure and to prove to me how happy they were to see me return safe and sound after so many misfortunes and so long an absence. Several people invited me to visit their homes and offered me family hospitality. But, before I had answered one such invitation another visitor would arrive. Then I expressed my thanks, excusing myself on the ground of my obligations to a people who had received me so cordially.

"Oh, well, tomorrow," they would then say. And why not spend a few days in Quebec?" ... In a word, everything that the liveliest interest and the greatest cordiality could suggest.

For myself, I was in a hurry to see my parents of whose fate, even at that very moment, I was unaware. The following day I hastened to put all my affairs in order, and the very same afternoon went aboard the steamer running between Quebec and Montreal.

I have just said that I was unaware of the fate of my oid parents. To tell the truth, I did not know whether they were still alive, not having received any news of them whilst away, and not having been able to discover any in Quebec, where they were not known. It was, therefore, with a heart full of joy mingled with anxiety that I ascended the course of the St. Lawrence to return to the paternal roof. I did not sleep during the night, which I passed walking up and down the deck, for the weather was beautifully fine; thousands of stars shone in the heavens, and the temperature was delightfully warm.

On arriving at Montreal, I heard good news of my parents.

They had been expecting me from day to day, informed as they had been by Mr. Fabre, who himself had received a letter from Mr. Roebuck, brought by the mail steamer from England to New York, which had beaten us by nearly three weeks. Anxious to return immediately to my own parish, situated twenty leagues from Montreal, I at once exerted all my efforts to perform a duty which I held sacred, namely, to ask the Canadian people to provide the funds for the return of my companions still in exile. I was engaged in writing a letter on this subject when I received a visit from Mr. Duvernay, owner of the newspaper, the *Minerva*. Mr. Duvernay was accompanied by Mr. Le Pailleur, one of my companions in exile, who had returned home nearly two years previously.

No visit could have been more timely, for it is well-known with what zeal and devotion Mr. Ludger Duvernay had served the cause of the exiles of 1838. I then made him acquainted with the subject of the letter that I was engaged in writing when he came in. He told me that the matter was an accomplished fact; that the subscriptions levied in all the parishes and towns of Lower Canada, and then paid in a lump sum into the hands of the Treasurer-General of the "Deliverance" Association, Mr. Fabre, were amply sufficient.

We proceeded then together to the house of Mr. Fabre, who received me with good will and courtesy; Mr. Fabre, to whose memory I am very particularly indebted. He told me that the relief funds were sufficient for all expenses, but that mistakes in the methods tried to transmit the current value of these sums to Australia had been made. I pointed out to Mr. Fabre the ways and means which my experience of affairs in New South Wales suggested to me.

May I be permitted to interpolate here the chronological order of events, so as to set down the details concerning the return of my exiled companions and to record an act of generosity which justice requires should not be passed over in silence. Fifteen or sixteen months after the day on which I met Messrs. Duvernay and Fabre, all my exiled companions had returned home, with the exception of one alone, Joseph Marceau[19], who, having married in Sydney, did not desire, or was not able, to return. Of fifty-eight of us when we went away, nearly nine years later fifty-five had returned.

Three of the thirteen exiles left behind me in Sydney arrived earlier than the others, and this is how. Immediately after my letters to Mr. Roebuck and my interview with Mr. Graham in London, I had hastened to write to one of my companions, Captain Morin, to inform him (and through his good offices, all the other Canadian exiles) that certain sums of money were deposited at their service in London; I promised them, in addition, on my arrival in Canada, to take all possible steps to obtain the sum necessary for their liberation. I promised them then to seek out someone there who would be willing to advance them the wherewithal to return to England, being assured that there they would find the means of paying these amounts advanced, and I gave them the name and address of Mr. Graham, trustee of the Canadian subscriptions.

Providence decreed that a generous Englishman should meet my compatriot when he received this letter from me. This gentleman, whose name I do not know, said then to my friend that, on the strength of my letter he would advance the sums necessary to pay the passages of three exiles as far as London, where the money advanced could be repaid out of the amounts deposited in the hands of Mr. Graham. The result was that the friend to whom I had written, Mr. Morin, and two of his companions, Mr. Morin, Junior, and Mr. Remi Pinsonneault, returned at once to England with their generous protector, who also quitted permanently New South Wales, as did many other businessmen at this period.

As I was not able to depart on the same day as I arrived at Montreal for Saint Polycarpe, my good parents' place of residence, I took advantage of the opportunity to visit and thank Mr. Lafontaine for the outstanding part he had taken in the proceedings on behalf of our compatriots to obtain the amnesty which permitted us to be reunited in our beloved Canada.

The following morning, I went on board the steamer going to the Cedars. We experienced some delays on the passage through the Beauharnais Canal, so that I did not reach the paternal roof till two o'clock a.m. Naturally everyone was in bed when I knocked at that door through which I had entered so many times, that I had not seen open for eight years and behind which were sheltered the authors of my being.

29

The Paternal Roof

Reader of my notes, put yourself in my place. Imagine that it is you who stands waiting upon this threshold, and you will understand how I felt.

I did not wait long, I assure, and there was no necessity to repeat twice the words, "It is I," addressed to my parents, for they rushed towards the door: "It's Xavier!" cried my mother, "it's Xavier!"-"It is he," repeated my father, "it is he." - "It is he, it is Xavier," repeated everyone in the house.

My beloved parents threw their arms round my neck, saying, "Yes, yes, it is our dear boy!"

The first moment of emotion having passed, I went down on my knees before my father to ask his blessing which he affectionately granted; then we all thanked God on my happy return.

It was the morning of the 14th September 1846.

Ah, how pleasant, on my return home, did I find Canadian customs, the sweet, good customs of my forefathers. So I shall bring these notes to a conclusion by a stroke which depicts perfectly the village life of our countryside, which at this moment offered in my view so striking and so consoling a contrast with the habits of the people with whom I had found myself in contact for eight years; a feature which converts into action this feeling of good neighbourliness, which makes those whom Providence decreed to live close to one another in the same corner of the earth look upon themselvs as all members of the same family, according to the old Canadian adage: "Who is there dearer than one's relatives unless it be one's neighbour?"

I was not present in the homes of my neighbours, but I know so well what took place there that I am certain that I can narrate it exactly.

The old men, who, as is well known, often get up at night in the homes of the farmers to light their pipes at the stove's door, the old men, in the houses adjacent to that of my father, when they saw the lights moving about in our home at this hour and knowing that I was expected at any moment, said to one another, "Look, Xavier Prieur has returned from exile. His folk must be very happy!"

Then the old people had wakened the hired hands and the daughters-in-law, saying to them, "Listen now, Xavier Prieur must have come home at little while ago. Lights are moving about at the Prieur's."

For some miles around, everyone had got out of bed.

"We must go and see him," said the men, leaving their beds and getting dressed.

"But perhaps that might disturb them," hesitatingly replied the women.

"Not at all; does one disturb his neighbours and his friends when he goes to celebrate with them the return of a son who has been absent for so many years? Come on, then."

Off then they set, tapping on the windows as they passed along the road and calling out: "Xavier Prieur has arrived. Aren't you others coming to see him?" for fear lest the people within were not alive to the news.

Half an hour after the time when I had stepped within my father's doorway, a large number of neighbours had gathered in the house. A few minutes later arrived their good-hearted womenfolk, timid and chilled with the cold, their heads and shoulders covered by their big woollen shawls.

With emotion I shook heartily the hands of this generous host of friends, and, one and all we yarned until five o'clock in the morning.

"This is only the beginning of what you have to tell us," our neighbours then said, "But the remainder must keep for another time, for you need rest."

Once again I kissed my parents, and retiring into the room where my bed had been made ready for several days, I said to myself with a feeling of indescribable happiness: "Yes, here I am, fortunately, back from Australia!"

It is good to be here, my Canada, parish of my birth. Here I find again my parents, the friends of my childhood and my youth. O God, full of kindness, blessed be. Thou!

F. X. PRIEUR.

END NOTES

1. This was not the Major Campbell who was later the representative of the Count de Rouville.

2. How times have changed, Since then a large number of the accused of those lays have been, or still are, public servants, distributed all over the rungs of the ladder, and their leading counsel, the Hon. M. Drummond, after having filled the highest political positions, is one of the judges of the Supreme Court of our country.

3. Madame Gauvin often spoke to us about her son who himself had been concerned in the insurrectionary measures and whom she had seen, in the preceding year take the road of exile. Madame Gamelin has since become the founder of the Convent of the Sisters of Providence at Montreal.

4. The sentences were couched in these terms: "That N- N- be hanged by the neck till he be dead, at such time and place as His Excellency the Lieutenant General, Commander of the Forces in the Provinces of Lower and Upper Canada, and Administrator of the Government of the said Province of Lower Canada, may appoint!"

5. AUTHOR'S FOOTNOTE. Here is this noble and touching letter, but one too which exhibits the excitement of the feelings prevailing at that period, and also his own unrealizable hopes.

Montreal Gaol,
14th February, at Eleven o'clock in the evening.

The public, and, my friends in particular, await perhaps a sincere declaration of my feelings; at the fatal hour which must sever us from the earth, opinions are always regarded and received with a greater degree of impartiality. The Christian man strips from himself, at this moment, the veil which has concealed many of his actions, so that he may be seen in the full light of day. Self-interest and passions die with his mortal remains. As for myself, on the eve of rendering up my spirit to its Creator, I wish to make known my feelings and thoughts. I would not take this action did I not fear that my feelings might be represented in a false light. We know that the dead no longer speak, and the same reason of State which makes me expiate on the scaffold my political conduct, could very well fabricate stories concerning my attitude. I have both the time and the desire to forestall such inventions, and I do so in a manner true and solemn at this my last hour, not upon the gallows, surrounded by a stupid and blood-greedy mob, but in the silence and reveries of the cell. I die without remorse; I desired only the good of my country through insurrection and independence; my opinions and my actions were sincere, and have not been stained by any of the crimes which dishonour humanity, and which are only too common amidst the excitement of unloosed passions. Since I was seventeen or eighteen years of age, I have taken an active part in almost all of the popular measures, and always with conviction and sincerity. My efforts were for the independence of my fellow-countrymen; we have been unfortunate even until this very day. Death has already cut off several of my associates. Many lament in irons, a greater number are in a land of exile, with their property destroyed, their families abandoned without resources to the rigours of a Canadian winter. In spite of so many misfortunes, my heart still retains its courage and its hopes for the future; my friends and my children will see better days; they will be free; I have a definite prophetic feeling and a quiet conscience, both of which assure me that this will be so. It is this which fills me with joy, when all around me is desolation and grief. The wounds of my country will heal themselves, after the disasters of the anarchy which follows a bloody revolution. The peace-loving Canadian will see the rebirth of happiness and liberty on the St. Lawrence; everything contributes to this end, even the executions;

the blood and the tears shed upon the altar of liberty water to-day the roots of the tree from which will wave the flag marked with the two stars of the Canadas. I leave behind me children whose only heritage will be the memory of my misfortunes. Poor orphans, it is you whom I pity, it is you whom the bloody and despotic hand of martial law strikes clown through my death. You will never have known the sweetness and the privilege of embracing your father on clays of unhappiness, on days of festivity! When your reasoning powers permi.t you to reflect, you will see your father as one who, on the gallows, has paid for actions which have brought immortal fame to other and more fortunate men. Your father's crime arises from its failure; if success had accompanied his attempts, his actions would have been honoured with an honourable mention. "It is the crime but not the gallows that brings disgrace." Many men of merit superior to mine have beaten me in the unhappy race which I still have to run from the dark prison to the gallows. Poor children, you will have only a loving and disconsolate mother as your support; if my death and my sacrifices reduce you to poverty, beg sometimes in my name; I was never insensible to the woes of the unfortunate. As for my comrades, O people, my execution and that of my companions on the gallows" are valueless to you; may they prove to you that which you must expect from the English Government... I have not more than a few hours to live, and I have wished to divide this precious time between my religious duties and those due to my compatriots; for them I die upon the gallows and the infamous death of a murderer; for them I separate myself from my young children and from my wife, who has no other means of support; and for them I die exclaiming, "Long live liberty, long live independence."

CHEVALIER DE LORIMIER.

6. AUTHOR'S FOOTNOTE. Here is the exact copy of the two-page leaflet which was given by Hindenlang to his fellow-prisoners:

"Upon the scaffold raised by the hand of man, I declare that I die in the conviction of having worthily carried out my duty. The sentence by which I was condemned is an unjust one; I forgive wholeheartedly those who have carried it out. The cause for which I am being sacrificed is noble and grand; I am proud of it, and I have no fear of death. The blood shed will be washed away by blood, so that the responsibility for it will fall upon those who deserve it. Canadians, my last good-bye is this old cry of France: 'Long live Liberty, long live Liberty, long live Liberty.'

"Such are the last word which I shall utter upon the scaffold prior to my death.

C. HINDENLANG.

"Montreal Gaol, 15th February, 1839.

Two hours before my death."

7. Both Chevrefils and Louis Dumouchelle died during their term of transportation to New South Wales. They were probably buried in the old Devonshire Street Cemetery, now the site of the Sydney Central Railway Station. All the other transportees to N.S.W. except Joseph Marceau, who married and remained in the colony, returned to Canada.

8. A complete Biographical Dictionary of the "Patriotes," begun by the late well-known Canadian historian, M. Aegidius Fanteux, is now being completed by a Committee of the Montreal Historical Society, under the direction of M. Jean-Jacques Lefebre, Secretary of the Society, and Keeper of the Records of the Department of Justice, Montreal.

9. "Warburton, England in the New World."

10. Father John Brady, who later became First Roman Catholic Bishop of Perth, Western Australia.

11. The original document, of which I have a copy, containing all these details in tabulated form, is in the Mitchell Library, Sydney.

12. Longbottom is a small peninsula in the Municipality of Burwood, lying between the present Concord and the Parramatta River. The three small bays which appear on modern maps, France Bay, Exile Bay and Canada Bay, commemorate the presence there of the French-Canadian exiles.

13. Henry Clinton Baddeley, whose address is given as Longbottom, according to the Register of St. John's Church, Parramatta, died 2nd March 1842, and was buried three days later. In

the *Sydney Morning Herald* of 4th June 1842, is the application for administration of his estate.

14. Author's Footnote: "Father Brady, being himself an Irishman, makes here a bitter gibe at the condition of his own beautiful, but unfortunate country."

15. Today the three little bays adjoining Longbottom are known as Exile Bay, Canada Bay and France Bay.

16. According to the official list, this was Leandro (or Leon) Ducharme, author of "Journal d'im Exile Politique aux Terres Australes," Montreal, 1845. See my translation, Sydney, 2020.

17. This was Pierre Hector Mariner, of Napierville, described as "*patron de navire*" aged 58 years.

18. John Arthur Roebuck, born at Madras, December, 1802, but brought up in Canada. M.P. for Bath, 1832, and for Sheffield, 1849, 1868, and 1874-1879. A Radical, he wrote *The Colonies of England* (1849). There is a *Life* by R. Leader (1897).

19. Joseph Marceau, a farmer, the only member of the group of "Patriots" who remained in Australia, was born at L'Arcadie, in the Province of Quebec, on 24th January 1806, the son of Jacques Marceau and Archange Bourgeois. By his first wife, who died before his departure for New South Wales, he had three children. After his second marriage to Mary Barrett in 1844, he settled at Dapto, in the Illawarra District of N.S.W., and died there on 8th June. 1883, aged 77 years, leaving eleven children, the last of whom, James, died recently (1947) at the age of 90 years. From him, whom I met in Sydney and Dapto, I received the portraits of his father and mother, reproduced in this volume. In *La Presse*, the French-Canadian newspaper published in Montreal, in the issue of 12th February 1948, is a three-column article devoted to Joseph Marceau and the Rebellion of 1839. See also my note to Ducharme, *Journal of a Political Exile in Australia*, p. 50, Tanguay; *Dictionnaire des familles Canadiennes*; *Le Canada*, Montreal, 20th August, 1947, and *La Patrie*, Montreal, 18th August, 1947.

www.ingramcontent.com/pod-product-compliance
Lightning Source LLC
Chambersburg PA
CBHW071444090426
42737CB00011B/1776